LOVE IS MY RELIGION

VOLUME 1

LOVE IS MY RELIGION

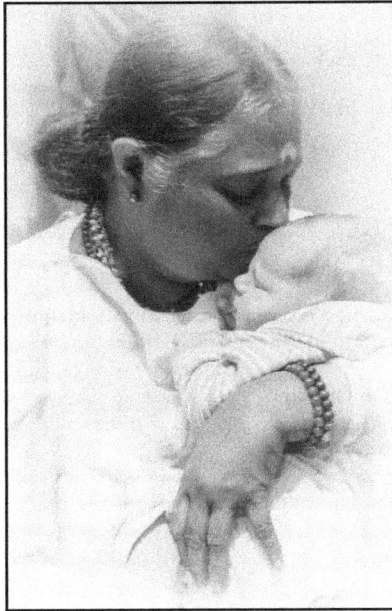

MATA AMRITANANDAMAYI

COMPILED BY JANINE CANAN MD

Love Is My Religion by Mata Amritanandamayi
compiled by Janine Canan MD
Copyright © 2019 by Mata Amritanandamayi Center
All rights reserved.
Except for the Introduction by Janine Canan, or for brief review,
no portion of this book may be reproduced, stored in a retrieval system,
transmitted in any form or by any means, or translated into any language,
without the written permission of the publisher.

Quotations in this book have been compiled from books, pamphlets, magazines,
films and songs published by Mata Amritanandamayi Math, India,
and Mata Amritanandamayi Center, USA;
from the web site www.Amritapuri.org, Amma's public talks and comments,
interviews and remarks to the editor.

Published by Mata Amritanandamayi Center
P.O. Box 613, San Ramon, California 95483
United States of America
www.amma.org
www.theammashop.org

First Printing: September 2019

ISBN-13: 978-1-68037-819-1

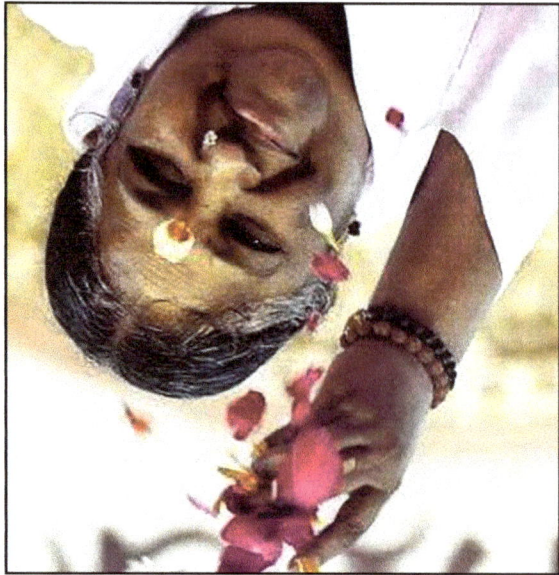

CONTENTS

*Photographs of Sri Mata Amritanandamayi
cover, title page, 6, 8, 26*

INTRODUCTION

Whose children are we, Mother, whose?
What is the purpose of this life we have been given?
Tell us, Mother, who we are, so we may dance in bliss.
Come, Mother, come, oh come! —Amma

For most people the experience of divinity is momentary and passing, extremely special and rare. But for the great Soul called Amma, it happens all the time. It is a permanent experience. For Her, everything is always God.

Who is this Amma, this "Mother" constantly privy to the power and mystery and grandeur of the entire universe? What an imposing question since her life extends far beyond the normal and ordinary. Sudhamani, as she was called by her parents, is said to have smiled rather than cried at birth. Neighbors in the small South Indian fishing village on a sandy peninsula amid quiet backwaters, humid coconut jungle and the encroaching Arabian Sea, could hear her singing to the gods as a very small child. Soon she was known as the strange girl who bathed the sick and elderly, and gave food and affection to the poor and hungry, even though her parents punished her severely for doing so. An uncannily gifted pupil, she was removed from school in fourth grade to manage a household of ten when her mother fell ill. The little girl worked from sunrise till midnight, often chanting holy songs and prayers. In her early teens, Sudhamani entered a state of bliss and spent a year living on the seashore, sometimes rolling in the sand or eating refuse in her ecstasy. Eventually, she experienced the visitation of the divine Mother and merged into Her. From then on, her powerful *Devi Bhava* ceremonies manifesting the divine Mother drew curious, larger and ever larger crowds. People began to call her Amma, which means "Mother." And her disciples bestowed the title Mata Amritanandamayi, "Mother of Immortal Bliss." *Amrit* refers to the nectar of the gods that confers immortality in the seemingly timeless mythology of India, or Bharat as it was originally called.

In 1987, Mata Amritanandamayi began traveling around the globe every year, visiting cities in Asia, Europe, North and South America, Australia and Africa, where She has given the transformative blessing of her loving embrace, her deeply attentive ear and her spiritual teachings, to almost forty million people—who have come looking for healing, love, salvation, knowledge and enlightenment.

Like one of India's immortal multi-armed Goddesses, Mata Amritanandamayi simultaneously guides Embracing the World, one of the most extensive charitable undertakings for the poor and needy in history—a network of projects staffed by thousands of volunteers, that provides food, clothing, housing, pensions, sanitation, sustainability, medical care in the form of hospitals, clinics and mobile units, as well as educational institutions including schools and colleges undertaking innovative humanistic research and providing scholarships. In India, Amma established the Clean India campaign, a wholesome television station, gender-inclusive temples, and a renaissance of traditional Indian art and medicine. Embracing the World sponsors global reforestation and natural disaster relief and sustainable villages. Substantial disaster aid following earthquakes, hurricane and tsunamis, has been provided to Haiti, Nepal, India, Japan, and the southern United States.

Amma's stamina can only be described as superhuman. Wherever She goes, this holy humanitarian radiates an irresistible beauty and enchantment. Her smile can light a stadium! For millions, Amma is the brightest light in a world increasingly harsh, threatening and violent. A living example of goodness, a miraculous embodiment of humility and compassion, a forgiving teacher who offers selfless love and spiritual sustenance, and a Mother to all—no wonder She is considered a sage of the first rank, a true incarnation of divine Motherhood and supreme Consciousness, a Soul that is one with Existence itself.

Amma's words and actions offer to humanity simple direct guidance in a world that we often find hard to understand and accept. Her message to the world is expressed in her life itself. Indeed She says that her life is her teaching. In the eyes of ordinary observers, it is one of incessant service, overwhelming compassion, unimaginable self-sacrifice, radical purity, immovable peace and bliss. Amma's is a life of pure Love. Small, dark, graceful, vibrant and jovial, draped in a simple white sari, Amma seldom rests or sleeps or has a moment to herself. "I do not have a life of my own—my life is for the world," She explains.

And where does all this energy and Love come from? "Amma and Creation are in an eternal embrace," She tells us. "I am like a river—I just flow...."

Over two and a half decades, I among many others, have had the extraordinary privilege and blessing of experiencing Amma in a wide variety of settings: on hillsides and beaches and under the stars, in churches, ashrams, temples, tents, hotels and stadiums, at the United Nations, at the Vatican, kneeling beside her chair enveloped in her arms—not to mention long distance, while meditating at home or lying in a hospital scanner. For me as a poet, Amma has been the inspiring embodiment of pure Beauty. As a psychiatrist, I have experienced Her as the selflessly loving Mother I wish all my patients had had—caring, laughing, warm and earthy, accepting as a river, strong as a mountain, radiant with unconditional love few of us have ever known—the kind of mother that glimmers in the rapidly fading, ancient matriarchal societies of the Keralans, Mosuo, Iroquois, Berbers and Bengalis, multiplied by unparalleled egolessness.

As a scrupulous, thirsty lifelong seeker, raised as a Presbyterian Christian, who has explored many religious traditions, I have found Amma to be the teacher who most surely holds the answers to Life's most important questions regarding our human purpose. In countless situations, at all hours, I have witnessed Amma doing nothing but selflessly giving. From a normal, egocentric perspective, it seems that what Amma is doing is impossible. And over the years I have come to see that doing the impossible is precisely her specialty. Amma insists that we are all capable of such selfless giving, that we are now using only a tiny amount of our human potential, that once we awaken to the Consciousness that is behind everything, and know ourselves and one another as part of That, it will be quite natural for us to treat others as ourselves—as Jesus taught two thousand years ago, and other spiritual masters have shown as well. Indeed, this loving Consciousness is the key, Amma says, and the only key to real happiness.

As the world watches Amma showering pure Love day and night, day after day, year after year, decade after decade, to everyone who comes before her, regardless of their age, sex, class, health, wealth, religion, education, achievement, moral development, or past actions—we are first bewildered, then stunned, overwhelmed and finally totally dumbfounded. Not only by the fact that this Love never stops—that is a supreme miracle in itself!—but also by the fact that it flows to absolutely everyone without exception. And we see for ourselves the bliss that Amma experiences in offering it. Staying up all night with Her, maneuvering the congested crowds, we become tired, irritable, critical, dull, distracted, but at three o'clock in the morning after nine hours of answering questions, feeding us, singing with us, directing multiple service projects, and hugging a thousand seekers, Amma is fresh, engaged, sweet, funny and joyful. And when She leaves the hall, She will go on to read a tall stack of letters from those who turn to Her for help long-distance. At mass gatherings in populous India, sacrificing all personal comfort, Amma may hug as many as a thousand people an hour for twelve hours or more, shining with Love and motherly concern. For She lives in an ever fresh present. The present is all there is, She says.

No one can do what Amma does, or ever has done, but She insists that we all have that capability. But developing it is a process that takes much time and patience, spiritual practice, and service to others—there are no short cuts. We do not need to believe in God, She says, as long as we serve others selflessly. Of course, She also states, "Saying you don't believe in God is like saying you don't have a tongue while you are speaking with it." Puzzled journalists, interviewing Amma while She is receiving long lines of people, often ask, "What is your religion? Are you trying to import Hinduism to the West?" Amma's answer is consistently: "My only religion is Love." And even as She speaks, She continues to practice her religion, gathering the next family into her mighty arms and boundless compassion. For her life is one unending gesture of Love.

To the damaged patriarchal world, Amma brings a fearless message of the feminine in all its fullness, bursting with beauty, intelligence and caring. Born into a culture that traditionally traced its ancestral line through the mother, and having attained a state of being that includes and transcends all cultures, Amma demonstrates the fundamental reverence and care for all Earth's creatures that all of us should feel and practice. It is a way of being that our world desperately needs to re-discover, before it is lost utterly in the machinery of selfish greed that has produced, in place of honor and respect, a devastating culture of male violence, feminine degradation, increasingly mechanical and heartless human beings, floundering, unnurtured children lacking moral values, and an exploited, devastated planet in crisis.

To men as well as women, Amma brings the teaching of universal Motherhood. To nonreligious rationalists and believers of every persuasion, She advocates the unification of science and spirituality on a solid foundation of compassion. She teaches us how to open our tightly closed hearts. And by the power of her example, her words, and her blessings, She slowly teaches us how to love.

Whether sitting under a tree during a tour across the Indian subcontinent; on the sandy shore of the Arabian Sea at her Amritapuri center; on the brightly lit stage of her free annual programs throughout America, Europe, Australia, Japan and Southeast Asia; in personal exchanges in airports, hotel ballrooms and ashrams; or at the Parliament of World Religions, the United Nations' 50th Anniversary Interfaith Celebration, the Alliance of Civilizations, the Global Peace Initiative of Women Religious and Spiritual Leaders, the Conference on Sustainability and Technology, or the Vatican's Declaration Against Human Trafficking and Slavery—Amma speaks in the ancient oral tradition and in her native Keralan tongue. To the Western ear, Malayalam is a direct, earthy, sometimes sultry or mournful, yet stately and ecstatic language—especially when sung by this great Soul in a searing voice that must wake up even the gods in heaven. Amma's numerous talks and songs, translated into a wide variety of languages by her dedicated translators, are available in numerous books, magazines, compact discs and videos, on television and the Internet. She has recorded over a thousand songs.

In the warm, immediate, tender tone of a mother, with the playful humor of a child, and the profoundly penetrating truthfulness of a true guru, Amma addresses her children about the centrality of Love in the life of humankind and all Creation. Her teachings do not mystify. They are clear, practical, explanatory, directive, even goading, yet reassuring, inspiring, comprehensive, brilliantly kaleidoscopic, and shockingly powerful. Amma's teachings are all encompassing. They teach us how to live life at every stage, and at every level of evolution—and they teach us why it is so important to live correctly, "dharmically," consciously, lovingly, in selfless service to Creation. I know of no other teaching more complete or timely.

Springing from the Source, there is a purity in her words, a gentleness, and a dazzling majesty that reflects the beauty, the energy, the genius, the sovereignty and the grace of Life itself. Each of Amma's talks is a kind of hologram of all you will need to know in this lifetime and beyond! Dipping into the infinite ocean of Knowledge, Amma gives us the full scoop. In pearl-strewn dialogues, seekers' burning questions are answered with rare thoroughness, from the loftiest plane to the most mundane—so that each answer can be heard at any level of understanding. No wonder this spiritual teacher is consulted by national presidents and prime ministers, prize-winning scientists, business executives, environmentalists, physicians, theologians, artists, experts from every field, as well as the poorest of the poor, the sickest of the sick and the broken hearted.

Of course, the sometimes deceptively simple, profound advice of this uniquely great Saint is not always easy to follow. Converting ideals into action takes work!

In these rapidly changing, ever more disorienting times, when all we have believed in and taken for granted seems to be melting before our eyes, like the glaciers and poles themselves; when plants, animals, even air and water are turning to dust—Amma encourages us never to abandon our goal of becoming truly human. And like magic, She touches our hearts with that possibility. The magic arises from her phenomenal yet very gritty life that demonstrates in epic proportions how to love, how to accept and help others, how to master ourselves and be truly free and happy. Everything in Creation changes, Amma keeps reminding us—for like little children, we keep forgetting. Our very bodies soon decay and disappear. So what can we really hold onto? Read on, for Amma's answers....

Love Is My Religion is a broad selection of core teachings and sayings from numerous talks and settings, both public and personal, gleaned over several decades, as the editor followed with ever-increasing awe this extraordinarily great humanitarian, revered spiritual leader and teacher, and exceedingly rare Soul. Here you will find a comprehensive sampling of her key instructions on attaining the immortal, the true, the beautiful, and the blissful. *Love Is My Religion* continues, expands and amplifies my earlier selections from Mother's voluminous oral teachings, *Messages from Amma: In the Language of the Heart,* published by Celestial Arts/Random House, "A Best Spiritual Book," in 2004, and *Garland of Love,* a pocketbook of 108 contemplations published in 2013 by the M. A. Center.

In these thousands of down-to-earth, powerfully revelatory messages to humanity, some quite recent—messages empowered to console and encourage, instruct and inspire, heal and illuminate us on our long arduous journey to becoming truly human—we find illuminations invaluable for our daily contemplation, our support in difficult times, and our long-term spiritual growth. Verbatim quotations are arranged around twenty-four themes that intend to amplify and clarify from a variety of angles, levels and moods, what this immortal Sage means by her often-repeated statement, "My religion is Love."

From the beloved Mother of Immortal Bliss, who shows us the feminine nature of the Cosmic Source of all things, pours a cascade of wisdom where we can quench our thirst for real knowledge. In these eternal waters the seeker can wade or bathe or—if very brave—dive all the way to the bottom. In the unfathomable and ineffable Reality that this supremely great Soul reveals, we can find the real gold that we have always been searching for, the most precious treasure of all—our own true resplendently shining and loving Self.

In the boundless and timeless flow of Amma's words and actions, we discover that the essential nature of Life and all that lives is simply Love. We find the answers to our pressing questions about the most worldly matters, instructions on how to live life meaningfully, successfully, joyfully, and with benefit to all—along with revelations touching upon the highest levels of Consciousness that point beyond language to the direct experience of divine Being Itself.

Amma's final word is the life of pure Love She lives from moment to moment in a cosmic drama that shows us how to live as Love too.

Om sakalagama sandoha shukti samputa mauktikayai namah,
Bowing to the Pearl inside the shell of all scripture,
Om Amriteswaryai namah,
Janine Canan MD

Amma bows down to all of you, who are the embodiments
of pure Love and supreme Consciousness.

Amma's words sparkle with ancient glimmers of supreme Truth.
They contain universal truths in hidden seminal form.
To understand them, the mind must be meditative.
—Swami Amritaswarupananda

To understand Mother's words,
it is not enough to read them with your intellect—
you also need to read them with your heart.
—Sri Mata Amritanandamayi

1

OUR ONENESS

Darling children,
we are all children of one Mother.

We are not isolated islands but are linked in a common chain
like beads on a single strand of Love.

Universal Love holds everything together.
It sustains and supports the entire cosmos.

Love is the center-point of life.
Life and Love are inseparable and indistinguishable.
They are one.

Love is the power that creates life.

Love is the fundamental principle that manifests in the beauty,
the vitality and the magnetism of life.

In the language of science, Love is energy—
pure subtle energy.

The same Life Force that pulses in the trees, the plants and the animals
pulses in every human being.
The same energy that gives people the power to speak and sing
makes the birds warble and the lions roar.
The same Consciousness that flows through us
moves the winds and the rivers, and illuminates the Sun.

Everything in life is alive and conscious—
but this great truth cannot be proven in the narrow confines
of the human mind, intellect, or language.

The whole cosmos is a vast interconnected network
that partakes of universal Consciousness.

Consciousness unites everything.

There is a precise, definite relationship between the cosmos and all of life.
Everything is harmoniously interconnected and has a purpose.
Amma says, there is harmony in the universe.

Nothing is insignificant.

The universe is like a net held by each of us.
When one part is shaken, it sends ripples throughout the whole.
Everything we do, whether consciously or unconsciously, together or separately,
vibrates to the farthest reaches of the universe.

Everything we do consciously has an effect.
Even actions that we perform unconsciously bear fruit.

Whether we are aware of it or not,
everything we think and do as an individual or a collective
reverberates through all of Creation.

We are one Consciousness.

Nothing in this world is insentient.

We can feel the pain of the smallest of living creatures.

Everything in Creation—wind, rain, ocean waves,
our own breath and heartbeat—has a rhythm.
Our thoughts and actions create the rhythm and melody of our lives.
When our thoughts lose their rhythm, our actions are affected,
and they, in turn, affect the whole rhythm of life.

There is no need to wait for others to change because when we change,
others are affected and they change too.

Humanity and Nature, Creator and Creation, inside and outside, are inseparable.

For God, the all-pervading divine Consciousness that is everywhere,
there is no such thing as inner and outer.

Everything is a manifestation of Supreme Being.

Just as ocean waves are always ocean and gold jewelry is always gold,
the Supreme dwells in everything on Earth—
and is not banished to the sky.

Supreme Being is the Consciousness that permeates all of existence.
It is not a person, it is Consciousness itself.

Whether it is in a necklace, a bracelet or a ring, gold is gold.
Everything in this world of innumerable forms is supreme Consciousness.

There is no difference between the water in the wave and the water in the ocean.
The Sun that shines on many pots of water is only one Sun.
We may see a thousand suns reflected in a thousand pots of water
but they are all the same Sun.

In form there is formlessness, and in the formless there is form.
Pure Consciousness is timeless and changeless.
As forms come and go, Consciousness remains eternally the same.

Everything is perfect with Consciousness.

Creator and Creation are One.
Only when we realize this, can we understand what we are,
can we become aware of our real Self, and can our individual soul be liberated.

God, the Absolute beyond all names and forms,
appears in countless divine moods and shapes.

If the wind can appear as a gentle breeze, a strong wind or a violent storm—
in how many different forms might the force of God appear?
Who can ever describe the glory of God?

The Absolute is present everywhere, all-powerful and all-knowing.

There is nowhere that is not God, the sages say—nowhere.
Everywhere is God—everywhere.

Indeed, there is nothing in the universe but God.

Everything is permeated with supreme Consciousness.
And to know and experience this is our real purpose as human beings.

According to the ancient seers and sages of India, God dwells in all beings.
Everyone is an incarnation of supreme Consciousness.
Human beings and God, Creation and Creator are inseparable.
The Creator manifests as Creation in each of us.

The Eternal Way tells us that with effort,
all of us can realize the divinity that we inherently are,
and that the realization of our Oneness is in fact the very aim of life.

Sanatana Dharma, the Eternal Way, teaches us that everything is divine,
that there is nothing but God, and Creation and Creator are one.
Everything in Nature is worshipped because God is in everything.
Our ancient prayer *Lokah samastah sukhino bhavantu* — May all beings be happy —
means that since everything is an expression of God,
we should always serve one another.

God is within us all and we are all within God.
Nothing is greater than seeing and worshipping God in everyone.
Once we grasp this subtle truth, how can we ever see anyone as different?

The Eternal Way teaches us to love and respect everything in this world.
It welcomes everyone like a kind and loving mother and turns no one away.
Anyone who follows and practices this path can reach the ultimate Truth.

In loving and serving others we make an offering to the Supreme Being.
Love, at any time and in any place, is an act of spiritual devotion.

We should see life as a sacred ritual and all our actions as worship.
We should accept everything as a blessing and realize that everyone and everything,
whether praised or blamed, is a manifestation of divinity.
This is the true meaning of *Advaita,* or non-duality.

We should cultivate the ability to accept everything as divine grace
and see the imperfections of others as reflections of our own.
Living life as a sacred ritual means seeing everything as holy.
This may be difficult at first, but eventually we will experience the Oneness.

Once we understand that we are permeated with pure Being
and our hearts are already full, we cannot hate ourselves, only love ourselves.

Love is natural—it is our real nature.

Love is not complicated—it is simple and spontaneous!

Love does not get tired or bored—grounded in Love, how can we be bored?

Love fills our hearts with more and more energy.
It refreshes and restores life.

Love is the very breath of the soul.
Love is the inner force that brings the living together
and makes all of us one.

Love is our very essence.
Love knows no boundary of race, religion, class or nationality.
We are all pearls strung on the same thread of Love.

We do not stop breathing among people who are not family or friends.
Love does not stop either among people of a different race, religion, class or nationality.
May we learn to love all equally since we are truly all One.

Everyone in this world is one in God.

We are all God's children.

Everything is one Consciousness.
We ought to see everything as inseparable from ourselves.
Awareness of our Oneness banishes loneliness, depression,
fear, sorrow and delusion.

Once we understand that all Love—whether for spouses, children, pets or plants—
derives from the same divine Source, we will glow like the Moon.

The goal of life is to realize our fundamental oneness with each other and God.

Only by feeling this in our hearts and putting this into practice,
can we ever be happy and content.

Each of us is outwardly different and made for a special purpose.
To avoid becoming self-centered, we need to join
and create a bright multi-colored rainbow.

When we do something just to satisfy our own desires,
we may do anything, even commit a crime—we see the other as the enemy.
We are competitive and uninspired in our effort.
But united, we make our best effort.

It is so important to become aware of our Oneness.

Come quickly, darling children, you who are the essence of OM.
Abandon sorrow and become adorable, one with the sacred OM.

In essence we are all one—children of one Mother.

The ocean waves roll over one another in a perfect circle—all one.
Universe, God and I—are all the same.

To spread the Love that is our true nature is the aim of human existence.

May Mother's children unite and shine like luminous rainbows in the sky—
like ocean waves caressing the feet of God.

May we grow and flourish as one family united in Love.

2

POVERTY OF LOVE

We are born for Love, we live for Love and we die for Love.
But today, there is a worldwide famine of Love.

Most people thirst for Love.

Modern history is characterized by poverty of Love.
More than anything we need Love.

There are two types of poverty: poverty of basic material needs
such as food, clothing and shelter, and poverty of Love.

Amma considers Love primary since it is what moves us to respond to others' needs.
When we feel Love and compassion we spontaneously and wholeheartedly
reach out to those in need.

Today's world is ruled by selfishness, lust, hate and increasing self-interest—not Love.
The wealth of Love we used to possess has been eroded by our love of wealth.

People today want luxuries, not necessities.
Coming into a large amount of money, people turn greedy
and feel they still do not have enough.

We never feel satisfied with what we have.
People used to feel compassion for other people
and take only what they needed—today the culture of taking
what we need and sharing the rest is rapidly vanishing.

In my childhood and youth, people thought about what they could do for others.
My mother taught me to save food for families with hungry children
and make sure they ate first—that culture is almost gone!
Today we actually do the opposite—
we sweep our dirt into our neighbor's yard.

Hindu scriptures say that we should desire for others
what we desire for ourselves—and try to make others happy not unhappy.
Christ taught we should love our enemies as ourselves.
The Koran says we should care for our enemy's donkey when it falls sick.
But we no longer believe in this ancient wisdom—
blinded by ego, we have no compassion.

We live in an age when the human bond has been greatly weakened.
Husband and wife, parent and child, teacher and student,
neighbor and neighbor grow increasingly distant.
All our relationships are failing.

We want everyone to love us, but do we love everyone? — No!
Sometimes we are fond of someone who does not care for us,
or someone cares for us but we are indifferent, even hostile, to them.
Loving only a few and expecting them to love us causes so much suffering.

There are seven billion people on this planet
but almost no one thinks about anyone but themselves.
Friendship, family, community are dead.
We have strayed from the herd like rampaging rogue elephants.

Parents live selfishly and care only about themselves—
children seldom receive the love and reassurance they need.

Nowadays when three people live under the same roof,
they might as well live on three different islands.
They cannot cooperate because each is guided by one thought only: *Me.*

Authentic human bonding is rapidly vanishing.
Young people cannot distinguish between love and lust, which is often masked as love.
Many lose hope and resort to suicide—which is not the solution!

Love gives life to everything it touches
but lust turns everything it touches into a lifeless object.

Lust is a universal phenomenon but formerly people had a firm foundation
of moral values and self-control which is absent today.
The scant discrimination of today's youth vanishes when they turn to the Internet
in search of pornography to fuel their sexual fires.

Most people use others rather than relate to others with love and respect.

As we outmaneuver each other,
indifferent to whether we are exploiting one another,
our human values keep draining away.

Our love is shallow and rarely based on mutual care and concern.
How, then, can we ever expect to be happy?

To enjoy life we must be relaxed, but most of us are tense.
Worrying about work, status, and what others may think or say,
men no longer spend quiet time with their wives and children.
Engrossed in worldly affairs they are anxious, irritable, bored,
and constantly craving something new—a new house, car, television or relationship.
Unable to be happy with what they have, they focus on what they do not have.
Driven by desires, they live in the past and the future,
missing the present altogether.

Today people try to find peace in drugs and alcohol.
How many families have been destroyed by addiction?
Among the young the phenomenon of addiction is as serious as war.

In pursuit of material gains society has abandoned Love, morality and responsibility.
Sensory pleasures keep multiplying as peace and happiness keep diminishing.

Out of touch with our higher values, we have lost touch with our very selves.

Addicted to money and luxury, we have forgotten how to live.

We can fly like birds and swim like fish,
but we no longer know how to walk and live as human beings.

When Amma was a child her village had no clocks, but everyone had time.
Today there are many clocks but no one has time.

Today the Ego reigns supreme!
Walled off from each other, we focus on gratifying our own desires.
Most of childhood is spent in play, half of life in sleep,
and even when awake we are half-asleep.
And so we miss the festival of giving and sharing that life should be.

Dominated by the ego, we are walled off and sunk in private fantasies.

Most of us are victims of the ego—very few are kind and sensitive.

Couples fight until their partner's heart turns hard and impenetrable.

Many mouth loving words with impure intentions—
Love without selfish motive is rare.

Blinded by selfishness we have lost our good judgment
and our perceptions have become grossly distorted

Obsessed with its material aspects we have lost the beauty and vitality of life

Locked inside us is a world of unexplored treasure—we have the key
but do not want to open the door.

Our thoughts and feelings barricade the dazzling fortune.
We are blind to the cosmic flower within us.

This world is more beautiful than heaven, but man's mind—
plagued by the triple madness, Money, Sex and Drugs—has ruined everything.

Even if God had created a world of pure goodness, such extreme self-indulgence
on the part of man would surely have turned it into hell.

The world has degenerated so far that people no longer even know
what peace and harmony mean—this must change!

We have forgotten who we are, though we seem to remember everything else.
We will not allow the ancient Wisdom to rise from within us.

In the current Age of Intellect, Reason and Science,
feeling has been entirely neglected.

Around the world people say, "I have fallen in love"—"fallen" yes, into a love
that is selfish and materialistic.
If we have to fall, let it be from our heads into our hearts.

Without real Love, there is and can be no happiness.

If we depend excessively on the material, we will always be deeply disappointed.

Without real Love, life is a barren desert.

Love is not a chain of bondage—it is the very breath of life.

The root of all our problems, from the personal to the global, is lack of Love.
Love creates bonds and unity
while hatred and egotism divide both the individual and the world.

Look at our world, my children:
So many people are suffering in wretched pain,
so poor they cannot afford even one meal or painkiller —
while others throw away money on smoking, alcohol and costly clothing.

So many destitute people struggle for their next meal and a change of clothing.
Countless young people drop out of school because they cannot afford the fees.
Many people live under a leaking roof because they cannot pay for a new one.
So many are writhing in pain because they cannot afford needed medications.

The money that some spend on harmful, life-threatening drugs and alcohol
could eliminate all the suffering caused by human poverty.

More than two billion people live below the poverty line
and hundreds of millions are illiterate.
It is our duty to provide food and education for all.

If everyone in the world worked half an hour longer and gave their additional income to assist others, poor starving unhealthy people would not even exist.

The world's wealthiest ten percent could, if they wished, improve the living conditions of the world's poor and eliminate global poverty altogether.

The poorest of the poor are those who become rich by taking others' portion.

We should all try to share what we have.

A twenty-dollar watch tells time as well as one that costs ten thousand dollars.

There are two kinds of poverty in this world:
the poverty that is caused by lack of Love and kindness,
and the poverty caused by lack of food, clothing, shelter and other basics.
Amma emphasizes the first because when we have a loving heart,
we spontaneously feel compassion and are eager to share and reduce material poverty.

It is our compassion and willingness to share that will reduce world poverty.
If we learn to control our constant desire for sensory gratification,
our greed for others' resources will come to a halt.

No matter how rich we are, without Love and compassion
we are living in dire poverty.

It is crucial to make every effort to reawaken Love—
the inner power that brings humanity together.

Love is the wealth that unbeknownst to us we already possess!

We all need to work at nurturing Love—
without Love, life is a barren desert.

Without Love, there is no life.

Love is our true wealth.

Only Love has the power to enrich and revitalize our lives.

Just as the body needs food to survive and thrive, the soul needs Love—real Love.

Love constantly makes life novel and abundant.
When we have Love, nothing is old—everything is fresh and new.

Our real life savings is Love.
If we lose that, we are truly paupers.
Let us try to deposit more and more Love into our inner treasury.

Life is Love.
It is through the feeling of Love that we experience life.
Without Love, life is arid and empty.

Unless we water our hearts with tears of Love, there is no hope for us or the world.

Without Love, our actions are mechanical.
Let us not waste our lives acting mechanically.
A human being can love, express Love, live in Love, even be Love,
but a machine can only be mechanical.
A machine can do many of the things we do—sometimes even better
and more efficiently—yet nobody is inspired by a machine because it cannot love.

Make some space inside you for someone else—first for your spouse,
then your children, then other people in your community and society.

Life is meaningful only when we feel happy over the happiness
and well-being of others—not only ourselves.

Love is a holy mantra we must chant with our hearts, not only our lips.

Without Love and compassion the heart is useless as a closed parachute
and will never be able to save us.

Poverty of Love is the worst poverty of all.

We must all actively nurture Love within us.

In today's atmosphere we must focus intensely on finding the thread
of universal Love on which all Creation is woven.

Love is life and life is Love.
This has to be lived to be understood.
Fill your hearts with Love and pour It into everything you do.
Let this be your constant aim.

May Love rule—and all our problems be solved.

3

UNIVERSAL MOTHERHOOD

Motherhood is Love.
It is the very breath of life.

Motherhood is not simply giving birth to a child.
True motherhood is Love, compassion and selflessness.
Motherhood means giving oneself totally.

The maternal attitude is not limited only to biological mothers.
It is innate in all women and even men.

The Love of awakened Motherhood is something we feel not only for our own children,
but for all people, animals, plants, lands and waters—for all beings.

When we awaken to our capacity for Motherhood
every creature becomes our child.

When we become a mother we cannot help but feel Love, empathy and forgiveness—that is
why anyone who is patient and loving is called *motherly*.

The first true Love we experience in our life is our mother's Love.
A mother's Love is pure and unconditional.

The Love of the mother who brings us into the world is the foundation of every life.

A mother knows her child's heart and pours Love into it.
She teaches her child the most important lessons and corrects her child's mistakes.

The capacity for motherhood is the very fiber and foundation of womanhood.
Women are inherently mothers, the creators of life.
A woman's greatest strength lies in her motherly power to create and to give life.

Women are the power and the ground of our existence in this world
and women's responsibility is incalculable.
A mother has enormous influence over her children.

The Love that flows through a mother's milk determines the future of the world.

Children learn their first lessons of Love and patience from their mothers.

She who rocks the cradle holds the lamp that lights the world.

When we see people who are happy and peaceful, children who have fine qualities
and good characters, men strong in the face of adversity and failure,
people sympathetic, compassionate, kind and generous,
we usually find that a great Mother has inspired them to become what they are.
A woman whose motherly nature is alive creates heaven
and brings peace and happiness wherever she goes.

If women forget their true inner nature, heaven will vanish entirely from the earth.
The world will become a living hell—
the human mind and the planet both reduced to a battlefield.

Woman is humanity's first guru, guide and mentor.

If women abandon the feminine principle
they will collapse and society will collapse with them.
The problems of the world will not be solved but exacerbated.

Amma is trying to re-awaken the true sense of Motherhood
precisely because it is so desperately lacking.

In the West, touted as the land of the intellectual, many people
are emotionally disturbed due to lack of motherly Love.

Our greatest need in the world today is the actualization
of every woman's mother-potential.

We urgently need what women have to offer!
Women must act from the deepest roots of their inherently maternal nature.

If women, in developing their masculine qualities, reject their feminine qualities
the extreme imbalance now threatening the world will greatly worsen.

For women awakening means identifying with and developing the pure power
of Motherhood which they already possess.

In women we find many powers rarely found in men.
Women can do many different things simultaneously, beautifully and even perfectly.
The fluid streaming energy of the Feminine makes it easy for a woman to be both wife,
mother, friend, advisor and guide, and also to conduct a career.

As a mother a woman plays many roles — she has to be both warm and tender,
strong and protective, and able to discipline her children.

Mother-power enables a woman to be reflective as well as responsive.
While males tend to be less reflective and more reactive,
the female mind is able to reflect and respond simultaneously.

A man's only role in the birth of a child is the offering of seed
in a moment of pleasure—for a woman birth means nine months of austerities.

Every child begins inside its mother's womb as part of her body.
The mother creates the most hospitable environment for life to grow in her
and then gives birth to that life.
How can anyone possibly justify saying that woman,
who gives birth to man, is his inferior?

The principle of Motherhood is vast and powerful as the universe itself.
Supreme Being is genderless,
but if It had a gender, It would have to be female
since he is contained within She.

A woman should always base her actions on the maternal qualities
Nature has so graciously bestowed upon her.

The capacity for Love and patience is natural in a woman.

Women's Love, compassion and patience is the only thing that can reduce
the hyperactivity and aggression of men.

Today's world, created by and for men,
does not consider the wants and needs of women.
Women have to establish their own identity and recreate society.

In this toxic artificial world, women need to protect their maternal abilities
very carefully from contamination and distortion.

The most urgent need of our time is for the maximum contribution of women!
This means that women must cultivate both their maternal and masculine abilities.

Women should venture into every area of society with confidence
in their inherent Mother power — otherwise, their actions
will hamper not hasten human progress.

Striving for their rightful place in society
women must not abandon their true nature!
Women need to be extremely careful not to lose themselves —
which is, unfortunately, a growing global trend
that will never help them become free.

If women reject their feminine nature and try to become like men,
the imbalance in the world will become even greater — the very last thing we need!
What we need is the maximum contribution of women to society.
We need universal Motherhood.

The world urgently needs what women have to offer.

Today patience is a sparse commodity.
When competition and hostility are the norm, it is women's patience
and tolerance that create what little harmony remains.

If women lose touch with their real selves, there will be no harmony at all
and destruction will be unleashed on the world.

To save the world it is mandatory that women make every effort
to rediscover their basic nature.

Women will never gain real freedom by imitating men!
The source of women's freedom and empowerment lies within them.

Women should never feel inferior to men.
Women have given birth to every single man in this world
and should be proud of their unique blessing and have faith in their divine Power.

The Creator gave the boon of Motherhood to women alone.
If this is lost, everything else will be meaningless.
Women should never lose their patience—for it is the very thing that keeps society stable
and gives women the Power to resurrect nations.

Women are responsible for Creation and are born
with the capacity to be patient and loving.

A woman's inner strength is like a river
that can overcome any obstacle in its way.

With the power of Motherhood, a woman can influence the entire world.
Women should not think about what they can gain from society
but what they can give!

Once she is awake, a woman can contribute whatever she wishes
and obtain whatever she needs.

For the collective growth of society men must open their minds,
accept and encourage women and acknowledge their special strengths.

Women are not decorations created for men's pleasure
or objects meant to be controlled by them.

Women should not be kept like potted plants—
kept from growing to their full stature.

When women are denied their rightful social status,
the whole world is denied their unique and crucial contribution.
Men should step out of women's way—
indeed, they should make way for women's progress.
A man should never block a woman's advancement toward her rightful place.
Men need to realize that the full contribution of women is absolutely vital to the world.

Men have suffered from the exile of the feminine principle, as well as women.

The oppression of women and the suppression of the feminine in men
has painfully fractured all our lives.

As an electrical circuit depends on both a positive and a negative pole,
the flow of life itself depends upon men and women playing their respective roles.

In marriage a man and a woman should be like the two wings of a bird.

Unfortunately, today men still feel great resistance to really understanding,
accepting and recognizing women and the feminine side of life.

Some men, Amma has observed, do not really pay attention to what women say.
Considering women weak, they act as if women's words were worthless.

After ten thousand years of history, woman's social status is still second to man's.

Degrading strictures, superstitions and primitive customs designed by men

to exploit and subjugate women still prevail all over the world.
Women need to break loose from this magnetic field—shake it all off and wake up!

Most women are still asleep—awakening this sleeping Power
is one of the most critical needs of our time, and not only in developing countries.
Women in materialistic secular societies need to awaken to spiritual consciousness,
while women in restrictive religious societies need to awaken to modern thinking.

Only when women have integrated modern education
with timeless spiritual principles, will they realize their enormous Power
and be ready to take action.
Women must find their courage!
They should not rust away inside the four walls of the kitchen
but step out, offer their talents, and realize their goals.

Women must wake up and rise!
If women do not make this effort, they are in a sense
responsible for their own confinement.

Women must be courageous and stand up for their rights—which does not mean running away from their responsibilities as wife and mother.

For pure female Power to emerge, women must acknowledge their weaknesses and conquer them through willpower, service and spiritual practice.

When girls are young and impressionable, their mothers need to teach them to be fearless and strong-hearted.

Boys and girls should be treated equally.

Mothers must firmly tell their young daughters to be courageous and brave and never let anyone belittle or insult them.
Parents should teach their sons to protect and respect women and treat them with kindness and empathy.

Men commit by far most of the crimes and killings in the world.

The destruction of Nature and men's attitude toward women are deeply related.
Nature holds the same place in our heart as our mother.

Women need to cultivate their masculine qualities.
Men to cultivate their feminine qualities.
Everyone needs both courage and compassion.

Some societies believe in totally covering up women
yet still breed harassment, molestation and rape—which proves that the problem
is not external but in the minds of men.
Governments can change as many laws as they wish
and institute harsh sentences for sex offenders, but only when we raise our children
with correct moral values will there be any real change.

Rape crimes arise from depraved minds—out of frustration, hatred,
intense lust and the psychological need to dominate.

Men still believe they are physically and mentally superior to women.

The arrogant and misguided notion that women cannot function
without them is apparent in all their behavior.

Even in economically developed nations,
men still resist sharing political power with women.
We can count on our fingers the number of women who have succeeded in politics.

Men are conditioned to demean and condemn women's achievements
even though they are clearly not superior.
Nor are women superior to men.
The truth is, no one in Creation is superior to anyone else.
Men are like single-lane roads, that need to be widened into double-lane highways—
where women can move alongside them.

Women need to be courageous!
Based on her own experience, Amma can say that women have the Power
to successfully fight the systems blocking their progress.

Women can perform any task as well as, or better than, men.
Women possess willpower and creativity, and thanks to their combination
of intelligence and mental purity can reach extraordinary heights
in any field, especially spirituality.

Women are repositories of infinite Power.
With discrimination and determination, they can more easily
attain full realization than men.

Women have the capacity to listen to others' sorrows,
respond with compassion, and be as firm as any man.
But this very capacity also bestows a greater responsibility on women.

Women are responsible for Creation!

Women hold the reins of the family and sustain the integrity and unity of society.

Women have a moral responsibility to the world and themselves
to shoulder equal responsibility with men in society's growth and development.

Today we hear heated discussions in every sphere of society
about giving women equal representation
and according women equal respect and admiration.
This is a welcome sign of change.
Subjected to physical, emotional and intellectual exploitation and persecution,
women have suffered in silence, without dialogue, for too long.

We must restore to the world the nurturing Energy of the feminine!

Deep maternal feeling is rapidly vanishing from the Earth.
To realize the possibility of peace and harmony,
men and women must both cultivate feminine qualities.

The capacity for Motherhood exists in everyone.

To ensure harmony on Earth, *everyone* must cultivate a maternal way of being.

Men must awaken to the feminine and develop empathy for women and the world.
If men cultivate their feminine qualities, they too can become loving,
affectionate and maternal.

Remember, my children, if motherly Love is allowed to disappear,
it means the total downfall of our children and our country.

The coming age must be dedicated to reawakening the healing power of Motherhood!
Each of us must discover and actualize our capacity for faith, Love, patience
and sacrifice for the good of all—this is what Amma means by *Motherhood*.

Anyone with the courage to surpass the limits of the mind, can reach the state
of all-embracing Motherhood, of Love and compassion for all life
whether human, animal, plant, earth or water.

Universal Motherhood means Love that embraces all of Creation.
Once we awaken to that Love, which is our true nature, all of Creation is ours.

Seeing, loving, serving and worshipping everything in universal Motherhood
is the supreme Devotion.

In order for the future to be fragrant and beautiful,
women and men must hold hands in every sphere of life.

By acknowledging Supreme Being,
men and women can both become instruments of that Power.

When universal Motherhood awakens, Love and compassion for all beings
will be as much a part of our being as breathing.

True Motherhood is pure Love and pure Being.

May the coming age be dedicated to universal Motherhood.

4

A LOVING FAMILY

Love should begin in the family.

We are all God's children.
The individual soul belongs to God, the giver and taker of life—
any other way of viewing this is foolish.

Our spouses and our children do not belong to us,
nor do we not belong to them—everything belongs to God.

A child is a gift from God.

In the eyes of a child, we can see God.

Everything created by God is unique and special.

No two blades of grass, no two flower petals, much less two human beings,
are ever identical.
Our fingerprints, our faces, our eyes are all unique.

In every human being there is infinite potential.

Children need to be nurtured with Love and patience.

Just as the body requires food to grow, the soul requires Love.

Without Love a human being cannot develop.

It is vitally important for parents to give Love to their young.

Love is more nurturing even than a mother's milk.

Just as a sapling needs to be watered to survive,
a child needs painstaking, tender, loving care.

Like a plant in a dark room reaching toward the sunlight,
a child naturally gravitates toward Love, attention and recognition.

When a mother feels her baby's vibrations, her breasts spontaneously leak milk—
this is how real Love responds.

Until children are five, they should simply be loved and allowed to play.
We need to make sure they do not hurt themselves
but should be loving regardless of their mischief.

We keep forgetting that Love is the foundation of a happy life.
Love that is not expressed in words and actions is useless.

What use is honey hidden in a stone?

Love can only be experienced by expressing it!

Express your love clearly, my children.

A home needs Love to give it life, or it will become hell.

When children get into trouble, we should explain matters lovingly.
The foundation of life is set in childhood—if parents do not give their children
enough Love and attention, they easily go astray.

Projecting our defects onto our children can stunt their growth
and cause them to close their hearts
to giving and receiving Love.

It is so important to share our Love with our children.

We pay for their cars and motorcycles and higher education,
but if we do not nourish them with Love and supplement Love with meaningful values,
they will never grow strong enough to give and receive Love.
Love and moral values teach children how to give and receive Love.

A child's first teacher is its mother.
Everything depends upon how the mother trains her child.

Love speaks in kind and gentle words.

Love does not complain or criticize.
Love is not aggressive.

Forcing children to obey only provokes hostility and retaliation.

All children were once part of their mother and totally identified with her.
The maternal bond is very strong, and it is what gives children the inner strength
to avoid succumbing to modern ills like drug addiction.

The Love and positive values that parents give to their children
are the greatest assets that their children will have
for facing life's unavoidable challenges.

Love and money alone are not enough.

Children need Love and attention to grow strong.
Outside information accessible to the young today means that discipline and Love must
go firmly hand and hand.

Parents should be aware of the dangers of giving their children everything they ask for.
They should give wisely and teach their children to use their possessions properly.

The riches that parents really need to give their children
are culture and morality.

Without Love and moral values, a child is like a car without a battery—

it can neither start up, nor advance.

Our parents are our first teachers
and it is crucial that their words and deeds set a positive example.

Children imitate their parents.

Good values are instilled by example—in the same way that we make yoghurt,
stirring a little starter into the fresh milk and letting it sit.

A child's mind is like freshly laid cement—footprints remain forever.

Just as a pot can easily be made when the clay is wet,
a child can easily be shaped when still fresh and impressionable.

Good thoughts and values imprinted in the mind of a child will last for a lifetime.

Parents have great influence over their children.
If they are moral, their children will be moral too.

Telling young children about the great Souls
and the importance of being compassionate is critical.
If we bring up our children to be strongly rooted in true values—
the timeless virtues accepted all over the world—they will behave accordingly.

Creating a path in soft fresh grass requires walking through it just a few times.
Once the grass grows tough, it is hard to make a new path.
Children are easily molded when young—later on, it is very difficult.

Nearly all the influences determining a person's mental health
arise from family environment.
Seventy percent of the foundation of a child's growth is laid down by age eight or nine;
by age ten, the fundamental lessons have been learned.
The rest of mental growth is built on these strengths and weaknesses.

Building a skyscraper requires a strong foundation.
Positive values should be nurtured from the very beginning of a child's life.

The world has changed enormously in the past three decades.
Not only have we stopped fulfilling our duties, we have forgotten what they are.

Children need to be taught the importance of cleanliness from an early age.

Children need to be taught to love and respect their elders.

If we do not care for our parents, our children will not care for us.

The Love we receive is proportional to the Love we give.

Only if we give Love, will we ever receive it.

Today, excessive social freedom is rapidly severing the crucial mother-child bond.
Children do not receive the maternal Love and protection they need,
and parents are deprived of their children's Love and company
and eventually exiled to lonely old-age homes.

How can sons and daughters ever forget their responsibility to the mother
who bore them inside her body for nine months, labored to bring them into the world,
let them wet her lap and wake her at any hour,
cuddling and loving them with unwavering patience.
We should reward our mothers with a warm embrace and honor our fathers as well.

We can never repay our birth mother for what she has given us
by carrying us in her womb and raising us through childhood.
At the very least, we should have the heart to console her,
share in her pains, love and honor her, and respond to her needs.

Indian culture teaches us to love and honor our parents as God.
It was always a son's duty to protect and care for his elderly parents.

Parents were equally devoted to their children, whose happiness was their own.
India's mothers were like trees, always providing protection —
even as they were being cut down.

A parent's ambition was the growth and success of their children
who were equally devoted to their parents' well-being.
Today as we witness the wrenching apart of this noble parent-child chain,
it becomes the duty of all to protect and strengthen it.

True freedom does not mean living any way we wish.
It means triumphing over selfishness.

While Westerners have more freedom than Easterners,
their hearts are dry and their minds teem with frustration and conflict.

Discipline is man-made — compassion is made by God.
We need both.

Western society has many freedoms but parents lack the right to rebuke
their own children, who often go astray as a result.
Raised with excessive freedom, children do not become strong enough
to handle life's challenges and obstacles.
Frustrated and disillusioned, many become emotionally disturbed.
Internally or externally, too much freedom is the route to prison.

We must reawaken in every heart the Love and responsibility of children to parents,
of individuals to culture and country, of students to teachers
and elders to the coming generations.

We should live our lives with Love, cooperation and tolerance,
and keep vigilant not to let the chain of Love break.
We should be like beads strung together on a single strand.

Only when families express Love to one another
does peace and harmony flourish in the home and in society.

Let us awaken from our stupor of selfishness!
Little acts of love and respect for our kin make us happy
and fill our hearts with joy.

It is very important to remind family members of their inner potential
and help them to realize it.

Today, husbands rarely console their weeping wives and children.
Wives rarely soothe their anxious, pressured husbands.
Ice will not help someone who is thirsty.
The right help has to be given at the right time
to create a sympathetic family environment.

Many men pay no attention whatsoever to what women say,
convinced that women are weak and their thoughts utterly worthless.
Women may not be perfect, but every human being needs Love and affection.
Husband and wife both need to listen.

Women tend to express their feelings and men to contain them.
Women express more affection and expect more in return.
Men should take the time to develop the patience to listen
and should not expect women to be like men!
Men should not view women as mere objects of pleasure or as maids.
Women too have minds and need Love.
Women should try to empathize with the hearts of men as well.

Husbands and wives both naturally long for Love,
but foolishly they approach each other like beggars.
They do not express their Love—
but Love must be expressed!

Neither male nor female should be placed on a pedestal—
each has their own special place.

Marriage should be a solution to individual inadequacy, not a competition for power.
Men and women were not made to compete but to complete and support each other—
to journey together and evolve toward Self-perfection.

Married life should be seen as a path to realize the true Self.

As long as neither partner has reached perfection, each should compensate for,
not emphasize and criticize the other's shortcomings.
With real Love comes sacrifice, the willingness to sacrifice
our personal preferences for the other.
This is the true spirit of marriage.

Marriage is an excellent way to learn patience, unselfishness and humility.

Husband and wife should live not as two, but as one.

The relationship between wife and husband should be like a pair of eyes.

A marriage of Love and mutual understanding
will naturally awaken the feminine qualities in a man
and the masculine qualities in a woman.

Only Love rooted in mutual understanding will evolve
into the kind of Love that does not change with changing circumstances.

Mutual respect and understanding must be the very fiber of family and social life.

When the hearts of wife and husband are united, the family will be stable.

When we have real Love and devotion, we will not get tired and bored.
Like a mother caring for her child, we will not feel burdened.

Real Love is beyond likes and dislikes and involves self-sacrifice.

When there is real Love, self-sacrifice is automatic.

When there is real Love and devotion, two do not exist.
You and *I* dissolve and there is only Love.

Real Love gives everything without any thought of receiving.

Real Love expects nothing and gives everything.

Real Love is kind and thoughtful.

Real Love accepts others as they are.

Real Love forgives and forgets.

Real Love overcomes every obstacle.

Real Love creates happy smiling faces and caring hearts.
Real Love keeps life in balance.

Let us fill our hearts with Love and express it in everything we do.

Once we realize that our Love for our spouse, children, animals and plants
derives from a single divine Source, we will glow like the Moon.
This Knowledge is what creates stability and harmony
in the life of the family and society as a whole.

Love is the foundation of a joyful life.

5

TRUE EDUCATION

There is infinite potential in everyone.
To awaken this dormant power is the true purpose of education.

God sends everyone to Earth with a special hidden ability
and a purpose only he or she can fulfill—this is what makes life
a joyful and meaningful communion.

Our talents and abilities are the treasures given to us and the world by our Creator.
Life's greatest tragedy is not death but neglect and waste of our gifts.

There are two types of education:
Education that teaches us how to earn a living
and education that teaches us how to live.

Education that teaches us how to live
provides knowledge about life, the mind and the heart.
A full education means understanding ourselves, as well as the world.
From childhood on, we should be learning all about life
and how to make it happy and fulfilling.

Real education is not merely a tool for achieving a comfortable life-style!
When plans collapse in failure and loss, education should help us
regain our balance, our confidence and our hope.

Knowledge without basic spiritual principles has no foundation.

Spirituality offers us a deeper knowledge of the world, the mind and the emotions.
It teaches us how to live well and focus on what is most important—our true Self.

Universal spiritual values are the foundation of every society
and without them society easily crumbles in conflict and hostility.

We constantly tell our children to *study, study, study,*
but they need to be taught moral values as well.

Contemporary education emphasizes development of a strong ego.
Confidence is important but the ego should not be encouraged.
We see the Moon because it reflects the Sun,
not because of anything we do—we should be humble.

Within us there is a storehouse of sacred Knowledge.
But only with a reverent attitude can we open its doors.

Today's students have no idea why they study.
Untaught and mechanical, they lack moral values and respect for their teachers.
Before their impenetrable walls teachers turn robotic
and heart to heart communication is utterly lost.

The only reason that children study today is to get a good job,
not to learn and develop as human beings.

Our educational system has been reduced to a mere tool for achieving material success.

Contemporary education has turned human beings into walking computers
and well-dressed, heartless corpses.
Addicted to fashion and gadgets, the young live in a world
reduced to only themselves and their things.
Most young people are physically unhealthy and mentally disabled.

To the three monkeys whose hands cover their eyes, ears and mouth,
Amma feels we need to add a fourth—whose hands cover his cell phone.

We no longer value seeing each other face to face.

The life of children today is very different from what it used to be.
Many are sent to school when too young and only experience tension.
We have put worms into buds that could have been beautiful flowers.

Our children's minds have been stunted by the heavy load
they have been forced to carry.
Parents need wisdom and the ability to communicate it.
Material education may help our young find a job and fill their stomach—
but this is not enough!

As educational standards keep rising higher, our values keep plunging lower.
Our education is like an airplane spinning out of control in outer space.

How far we have deviated from our values—how much we have lost!

If good values are not taught to children when they are young,
the future will be populated by demons instead of humans and gods.
A demon's only thought is *I*.

Normally children pass through developmental stages—
turning over, crawling, walking—like soldiers who refuse to be defeated.
But today, from early on, children are like businessmen.

Everything is a deal, even a relationship.
Other people's feelings and well-being do not matter.

A business mentality has taken over and all we care about
is what we can gain from any transaction.

Our houses may look impressive, but the families inside are in ruins.

Our schools and colleges are like battlefields, brawls and skirmishes routine.

Hatred and revenge have poisoned our hearts.

We live in an era of comfort that offers us no peace.

Who and what is responsible for this?
Society, parents, elders, schools, blind imitation
and a lifestyle with no regard for tradition and culture.

All of these have converged to create fear, anxiety and cowardice.

Human beings have become so weak that they no longer grasp
that life is an adventure—a challenge requiring courage!

The hallmarks of contemporary life are intense concern for physical security
and very little concern for spiritual security.

We sacrifice our values for the pleasures of life.
It takes a lot of time, patience and effort to cultivate values,
but it is easy to destroy them.

To build a culture takes long-term, conscientious effort, patience and persistence.
To demolish it, and not even realize it is crashing down, takes no effort at all.

Our country and our culture is our Mother.
Without her, we are like kites adrift on broken strings.

There is a growing distance between family members.
We live like islands—but we are not islands!
We are connected links in a chain.

Our educational system fails to convey the ethics and ideals that connect us
to Nature, community and society.

We have forgotten that the main purpose of education is the transmission
of culture, ideals and morality.
Education should spread the light of culture through its vision,
its ideas, its words and its deeds.

For a human being to develop, both mind and heart must be nourished.
Knowledge nourishes the intellect; meditation and contemplation nourish the heart.
A true education acknowledges the importance of both.

Today's education teaches the language of the machine not the heart.

Values have fallen by the wayside as education has become
merely a means of earning a living.
A true education includes the universal values of the heart.

Human beings have an inner as well as an outer existence.
There is no hope for humanity if we do not keep the two in balance.

To fully understand life, we need to be aware of both its visible and invisible aspects.

We need to live a balanced life of moderation—the middle path.

The intellect has grown so big, we need machines for everything—
even brushing our teeth.
We do not get physical exercise and have to schedule it.
We are always tense.
Comforts gained in certain areas have weakened us in others.

Our lives, especially those of the young, are consumed by unnecessary information.
Since young people believe only in the body and the mind,
they have become mechanical and selfish.

When we allow the mind to control us, we nurture our enemy.

Human beings are rapidly disappearing and being replaced by human machines.

Hyper-emphasis on skill has reduced the human being to a mere machine.

Worldly success is impermanent—along with outer success,
we need inner victory over the mind and the senses.

Current education teaches us how to think and analyze
but not how to stop thinking and be silent.

Young people, pick up the remote control for your mind!

We need mental discipline to help us become conscious.

Meditation practice is muscle training for the mind.

Handed down from the sages of ancient India, meditation is an invaluable gift
that helps us open ourselves to creativity, celebration and joy!

Meditation and contemplation offer a deeper kind of experience and knowledge.

Contemporary education inhibits our creativity by stressing material achievement.
And it deprives us of traditional values and wisdom.

We need education that imparts spiritual values,
love for society
and respect for knowledge itself.

Information should evolve into knowledge
and knowledge into discriminating intelligence.

When we over-identify with the mind and its thoughts,
we cannot be spontaneous—spontaneity comes from the heart.

The three steps to spontaneity are effort and hard work,
followed by forgetting our work and quietly experiencing the moment,
then allowing the intuitive mind to take over.
Intuition is spontaneity.

Intellectual prowess has its limits—it is very important
not to narrow the scope of education to the intellect!

Amma is not saying that we should not use our intellects
but that our intellects need to become discriminating.

Yes, we need intellect and reason,
but we should never allow them to devour our hearts.

The intellect is like a pair of scissors that cuts objects into pieces,
while the heart is like a needle that stitches them together.

The intellect speaks the distancing language of argumentation and aggression
while Love and service are what bring hearts together.

Reason kills the beauty and charm of life,
which is meant to be enjoyed, experienced, loved and felt!

Reason blocks Love.

Never try to rationalize Love—it is beyond logic.
Forget about *why* the river flows, the Moon glows, the breeze blows,
the sky is so wide, the sea is so deep,
the flower beautiful and fragrant.

Head and heart must join together and cooperate in every area of life.

Only when the mind and the heart function together can our actions be truly fruitful.

Study is a process that unfolds like a flower bud
slowly opening its petals into a beautiful fragrant blossom.
It takes Love and patience.

Success in life takes more than skill—
we need to understand our task and approach it with patience.
Life flourishes only with patience and perseverance.

Growth is always evolutionary—patience is necessary.

Patience is the foundation of all growth.
Haste never speeds up the process of growth—we have to be patient.

Patience, steady enthusiasm and firm determination
are the requirements for success.

Always be a beginner.
We need the humility, faith and patience of a child.
Only a beginner learns from their experience.
The mind can only expand to universality through childlike innocence.

Maturity is the ability to continue learning throughout life
and comes not with age but with growing selflessness and acceptance.

Children, may you mature without losing your innocence and your humility.
As your minds becomes more active, dynamic and strong,
may your emotions and feelings flourish too.

Young people are the scent of the future.
If our young do not develop into conscious, compassionate human beings,
the conditions of the world will only continue to deteriorate.

Faith and Love for Creation must be imparted to the young
through proper spiritually grounded education.
Not religion, but its spiritual essence must be taught in the classroom.

Spirituality is synonymous with universal human values
and any true education is founded upon them.

Just as food and sleep are necessary for a healthy body,
spiritual understanding is necessary for a healthy mind.

We need balance—the middle path—in our physical, mental and spiritual life.

We should lead a life of moderation and balance.

Education should provide the tools we need
to perform daily transactions, keep our bodies healthy and live a responsible life.
Education should teach the fundamental principles of life and death
and shine the light of culture via thought, word and action.

Knowledge and responsibility are the two sides of the coin of education.
Surely the goal of education is not to create a generation
that understands only machines.

Technology is a great servant
but a dangerous master.

We need culture *and* science.
Culture gives meaning and direction to life.
Science preserves culture and helps us meet our material needs.
Culture should be the eyes of science, and science should be the hands of culture.
Amma is happy to see her children's efforts bringing them together again.

In the old days games and arts were based on spiritual principles
and supported positive moral and cultural values.
Today's cinema, television and media are a threat to our culture.
To re-establish social harmony we need to revive spirituality in the arts
and every area of culture.

Our families and teachers are crucial in teaching children that their actions
affect others as much as the actions of others affect them.
There are consequences for everything we do.

Love, compassion, concern, honesty, truthfulness, humility and *forgiveness —*
the language of universal values is rapidly being forgotten.
Forgotten but fortunately not lost forever, since it remains deeply buried inside us.

We must show the younger generation the importance of Love, service and humility.

Schools should emphasize education of the heart in every subject.
Syllabuses should be full of lessons in Love.

Approaching young people with compassion can make a real difference.
We must set an inspiring example for our young.

Just as we stimulated our children's interest in making money,
we should stimulate their interest in protecting Nature.
Schools should teach environmental protection and provide practical guidance.

Community service should be compulsory for all students.
If schools require, organize and grade tree plantings and twice-weekly environmental
clean-ups, we can greatly alleviate the problem of pollution—
and simultaneously instill the spirit of service
while students are still young and impressionable.

Tomorrow's world will be shaped by today's children.
If spiritual principles are embedded in our educational system,
our children will become good kind human beings with strong minds and noble hearts.

We all need the booster rocket of spiritual values to avoid
being caught in the force of gravity.

The body is like a business enterprise and the soul is its profit.

The goal of human life is to fully realize the soul.
We should not forget the most important thing of all!

The light of Knowledge is here to drive away the darkness in our inner lives.

The teaching of universal principles and human values needs to be a standard part
of any general education and should not be left to the family alone.
We have no time to delay or future generations will be lost to the world.

In recent years Amma has seen a surge of spiritual eagerness from Westerners
who, increasingly unhappy and disillusioned with their freedoms,
have discovered that real freedom is internal not external.
Meanwhile, as more Westerners turn to spirituality,
Easterners are abandoning their own rich culture to follow the West
and sinking deeper into the world to consume the very pleasures Westerners reject.
It is important for Indians to know the basics of their own culture
and not have to learn them from books written by Westerners.

A true education is the ground of all positive change
and the secret of every truly successful life.

To soar high into the vast sky of spirituality, we need the wings
of service and devotion along with the tail of knowledge.

True Knowledge means accepting the world in its many forms
while remembering that a supreme Reality pervades it all.

May the young strive to understand and respect the power of supreme Consciousness.

May we always remember that one Power holds this diverse world together.
Education that teaches this broadens the mind,
expands the heart and spreads Love throughout Creation.

6

COMPASSION

Compassion is Love expressed in action.

When Love fills our hearts and flows out through our words and actions—
that is compassion.

Compassion is the language the blind can see and the deaf can hear.
Giving a helping hand to the lonely, food to the hungry or a caring glance
to the downcast is the language of Love.

Compassion is the perfume of Love.

We should sympathize with fellow human beings.
Compassion for the needy and suffering is our divine responsibility.

Only those who have experienced hunger really know how it feels—
only those who have carried heavy burdens know the strain.
It is our divine duty to show compassion.

If our minds, eyes, ears and hands could really understand and feel others' suffering,
how many suicides might have been prevented,
how many poor might have been fed, clothed and sheltered,
how many women selling their bodies for a living might have been helped,
how many sick in great pain might have received medical care,
how many wars for fame, fortune and power might have been avoided
and how many orphans found homes?

If we love God, we will certainly feel compassion for the suffering.

Consoling people in pain is true worship of God.
If we do not put compassion into our actions, Love is nothing more than a word.
If our hearts do not melt with compassion for others,
we cannot experience the feeling of real Love.

Kindness is the first step on the spiritual path.
Anyone with a kind heart does not need to go searching for God.
A compassionate heart is God's favorite place—God comes running!

Children, true Love and devotion to God means compassion for the poor and suffering.

We must feed the hungry, help the impoverished, console the grieving
and relieve their suffering.

The world needs not only words of sympathy
but hands eager to serve selflessly!

Each of us should spend at least half an hour a day

working for the poor and suffering.
Prayer is not enough—it needs to be combined with action.

Pure action is as important as prayer.

If we close our eyes to the world in the name of Spirituality,
our third eye will never open.

Children, just as you try to meditate with your eyes closed,
try to mediate with your eyes open too.

Meditation and action should be balanced.

Mediation does not mean simply sitting with your eyes closed.
Smiles, kind words and caring looks are part of meditation too.
In true meditation the heart is full of compassion
and the Self radiates light.

Just as food nourishes the body, charity nurtures the soul.

Meditation and scripture are the two sides of a coin
and service is the stamp that gives the coin its value.

We need to understand and share in the sorrows of others—
this is the right or dharmic attitude.
Only when our meditation includes compassion
does its precious gold become fragrant.

Consoling the sorrowful is a spiritual practice greater even than meditation.

The essence of true spirituality is service, forgiveness and self-sacrifice.
It is through our selfless actions that we awaken.

Service is the purpose of every action.

We are born to serve others.

We should be able to serve anyone, seeing God in them.

Sincere selfless work for society and humanity is the way to salvation and liberation.

Children, selfless service is the beginning and the end
of the quest for Self-realization—
and our most important duty.

This is how to serve the world:
See everything as a manifestation of pure Being.

Put down your sack of selfishness and lift up the sack of service!

We cannot avoid effort in either spiritual or worldly life.

But it is selflessness that invites the grace that makes life sweet and rewarding. Grace makes life full, complete and divinely fragrant.

A compassionate person enjoys the eternal compassion of God and the divine bliss of the Self.

May all your actions be an offering to the supreme Reality.

Serve others, especially the poor, with Love and expect nothing in return.

True spirituality is compassion in action.

Spiritual devotion and service are simply the two sides of the same coin.

All spiritual practices are intended to develop an attitude of devotion to this world.

Amma happily bows to anyone disinclined to do spiritual practice
who is fully dedicated to the world.
The same benefit received from prayer is received from selfless service.
In performing selfless action we become whole and our limited identity dissolves.

Not everyone can meditate constantly with singled-pointed concentration.
Therefore Amma recommends that people spend their free time
doing something good for the world and themselves.

Do not turn away from the cries of your sisters and brothers
but do what you can to relieve their pain.

The little we contribute can make a big difference!

When we see a blind man crying, instead of just feeling sorry
why not take his hand and help him across the street?
Instead of pitying the hungry, why not feed and help them to find food?

Let us think about what we can do for society.

A compassionate person is like a tree beside the road
that offers fruit to all who pass by.

Today, many have withdrawn into solitude and apathy
and are too busy to think of others.

Our biggest problem is that we do not think enough about others' problems.

Most people have only one mantra: *I... I... I....*

We exercise our bodies and neglect our hearts.

To be truly human, one must be able to feel the sorrow of others.
We are neither machines nor animals nor demons but human beings.
We should try to be loving and compassionate.

There is compassion in everyone—but we often find it hard to feel and express it.
Turn inward, go deep and ask yourself: "Is my heart alive—
can I feel the source of Love and compassion within me;
does my heart melt at the pain and sorrow of others?
Do I cry with the suffering and try to console them and wipe their tears?
Do I give food and clothing to the poor and hungry?"

Compassion is the unconditional Law of Creation.

Compassion is God.

We should all be the eyes and ears and hands of God.

We should feel everyone's pain and suffering as our own.
To accommodate everyone equally, our minds should be wide as the sky—
which takes the innocence of a child and true devotion to the Divine.

Our highest and most important duty in this world is to help our fellow beings.

The impulse to help others indicates a higher state of mind.

Love and compassion are the signs of an evolved life.
Only human beings can develop compassion and empathy.
Only by helping others can we evolve.

No other species has been given this precious gift:
the capacity to feel and understand.
We should use, not waste it.
If we refuse, the damage is lasting.
If we build a dam of ego, we block God's grace.

To communicate, people need to be able to read, write, speak and listen.
We are trained to read, write and speak but not to listen.

Most of us are very poor listeners.
Why were we given two ears and one mouth?
To listen twice as much as we speak.

To really hear we must listen.
When we really listen, speaker and listener become one.
A good listener learns from every experience,
responds appropriately, avoids unpleasantness and makes others happy.

Keen listening purifies the heart until it turns into a perfumery.

Listening is like saltwater that evaporates into the sky,
then condenses and falls in the rain and the snow.

Attentive listening is selfless service.

Let us learn to put others first.

Listen with your heart
and think before you speak!

It is not eyeliner that makes our eyes beautiful, but their caring glance.
It is not earrings that make our ears beautiful, but their ability to hear another's cry.

Life becomes meaningful when we find our own happiness
in the happiness and well-being of others.

When we share happiness it grows.
Sharing happiness is what makes the flower of life so beautiful and fragrant.

Every day, as we move through the world, we should do something
to make someone—a person or animal or Nature—happy.
We should try to bring somebody peace, pick up some litter, plant a flower seed
and feel the thrill of joy in our heart!

If we fail to serve, we should pray to Mother to give us an opportunity.

In this Age of Selfishness, selfless service is the only soap that can wash us clean.

Let us choose a path that helps others
and use our freedom for the betterment of society.

What makes Mother happy is to see her children making others happy.
Her children's service and devotion are like stars in the sky.

Every action should be permeated with the sweetness of Love,
otherwise it is nothing but labor.

We should fall in love with our work.

When we perform our duties with a cheerful open heart,

divine power and grace can flow through us freely.
Grace and openness are the same thing.

Find a place in your heart for others.
The seeds of spirituality sprout when they are watered with compassion.

A compassionate effort to help another will make your heart stronger.

Be passionate in your compassion—as if it were your own burning hand
you plunge into the cooling water.

Like a river rushing down a mountainside, a compassionate heart
gushes with Love and concern.

There are no rules for compassion.
Like water it flows everywhere.

A river flows only one way, but Love flows both ways.
A kind word, a caring glance, or a small favor that brightens another's life,
will also brighten yours.

Only by giving can we ever expect to receive.

Satisfaction always comes from giving, not from taking.

In the mirror of selfless service we can see our own true beauty.

It is not what we have that determines the value of our lives, but what we give.

The spirit of giving is the highest form of compassion.

If we do not put Love and compassion into our actions,
love is nothing more than a word.
If our hearts do not melt with compassion for others,

we will never experience real Love.
Love and service is the key that opens the door to the Soul.

Only if the Love within us finds outer expression will we ever be truly happy.
Take a vow to live a life of service.
Whether you believe in God does not matter
as long as you offer yourself in service to others.

As the Sun needs no light from a candle,
the Absolute, complete in Itself, needs nothing from us.
Supreme Being protects the universe by incarnating as compassion and Love
and dwells in the heart of all compassionate beings.

Compassion is the essence of Love.

Love gives to all without exception and expects nothing in exchange.

Be a giver, not a taker.
It is not important to accomplish "big" things.
It is more than enough to simply say a kind word, smile lovingly
and listen to another's problems patiently.

Life achievements — graduation, professional recognition and so on — have importance.
But our greatest achievements are the little things we do.
Consoling someone crying in misery, feeding someone who is hungry,
helping someone who has fallen — these seemingly small deeds
are greater than any public achievement.

To feel Love and compassion we need to become aware of the unified Life Force
that underlies and supports all Creation.

Compassion is the unconditional law of Creation.
It is the beginning, continuation and culmination of the individual,
society and the world.

A revival of the ancient language of Compassion can solve all our problems.
If we walked the path of our ancestors, we would easily find the solution
to our current state of affairs.

Let us cultivate the understanding that we are all One,
and as this understanding deepens
we will naturally feel more and more compassion and Love.

The first step in developing compassion is to approach so-called "inanimate" things,
like sand, stone, rock and wood, with Love, respect and empathy.
Then we will find it easier to feel compassion for the trees, vines, birds, mammals,
And finally, we will be able to feel compassion for human beings.

When we have compassion for others, our selfishness—
which is the greatest obstacle to the true Self—
spontaneously drops away.

We need to be able to see ourselves in everything that exists.
Allow yourself to experience everyone's pain and sorrow as your own.
Open your mind as wide as the sky
and with wide-eyed, child-like innocence embrace it all.

A compassionate person feels grateful.

At the heart of selfless service
is the state in which the individual self is forgotten
and others' pain and suffering is experienced as our own.
When we love others and see ourselves in them, we feel no hatred or fear.

When we approach the whole world with the attitude
this too is mine, our own problems fade away.

Compassion is the alpha and omega of spiritual life.

Compassion and selfless action eventually evolve into karma yoga,
which in turn leads us deeper into the Truth
and helps us to lift the veil of the ego and finally attain true freedom.

No religion or scripture is greater than comforting the sorrowful,
encouraging the weary, or offering a helping hand to those who are struggling.

To make others happy—even for a moment—is a very great thing!

When we share our happiness, it grows.
Sharing our happiness is what makes the flower of life so beautiful and fragrant.

It takes no money or special status to be compassionate.
A smile is invaluable and costs nothing.

Compassion is a choice.
We should decide to do some kind deed every day,
to love others as we love ourselves, and forgive others' mistakes we would as our own.
Sadly, smiles that flower from the heart and words that are fragrant with Love
are rare today—but nothing creates peace and calm better
than a sweet word or a loving smile.

The compassion we feel for those who are suffering eases their pain.

When compassion informs an action, it spreads waves that inevitably influence others.

The smallest action that we perform to help another has the power
to create a major social transformation.

The one-word solution to the problems of our world is *Compassion.*

If all of us placed others' needs before our own, the world would become paradise.

There is no greater power than Love and Compassion.
As our compassion grows, so does our inner power.

Never miss an opportunity to help someone.

Some people have not had the good fortune to know sweetness in their lives —
try to be understanding and share the sweetness
with which you have been blessed.

Whenever you eat a meal, remember the poor.

Food is tastiest when we eat only enough to satisfy our hunger.

Offering food and knowledge to people who need it, is our duty.

Those who have, should share.

Save a space in your heart for those who have less.

May what makes us happy be what makes others happy.
May we all be one heart full of Love, happiness and unity.

Find your own inner harmony —
the beautiful song of life and Love that is yours.
Go out, serve the suffering, learn to put others first, and take care
not to fall in love with your ego in the name of "service".

Be a role model of Compassion.
Compassion begins with small gestures.
A smile or a kind word goes a long way in spreading Love.

Fill every word, every look, every deed with kindness

and it will return to you as divine grace.

How many lives have we enriched with our Love and compassion?
These are the signs of a truly great person.

A compassionate person does not see faults and weaknesses,
or distinguish between good and bad in others.
When there is Love and Compassion, no line is drawn
between nations, faiths or religions.
Without ego there is no fear, lust or passion, and it is easy to forgive and forget.
Compassion is a channel through which everything flows without attachment.
Compassion is the fullest expression of pure Love.

Out of the muddy pond rises the beautiful fragrant lotus of compassion.

The glorious flower of compassion blossoms in the fullness of divine Love.

Divine Love is compassion for everything that exists.

Children, God is compassion.

Compassion in the unbroken law of life.

Our real nature is not selfishness—it is Love and compassion.
We must realize this and awaken to this truth!

We are mirrors that need to be dusted off
to expose the compassion that is our true nature.

Ultimate Power dwells in our compassionate hearts.

Know your Self.
Practice Love and compassion.

7

MOTHER NATURE

The Earth is our Mother.
We must never forget our responsibility to Her.

Nature is our first Mother
and she nurtures us our whole lives.
Our birth mother may let us sit on her lap for a few years—
even that is rare today—but Nature never stops bearing our weight.
Patiently she feeds and caresses us and sings us to sleep.

Just as we have an obligation to the mother who birthed us,
we have an obligation to Mother Nature.

Forgetting Her means forgetting ourselves.
Ignoring her means we are choosing the road to extinction.

Human beings are inseparable from Nature—
we are part of her and come from her basic elements.

Human beings, plants, animals, earth, sky, Sun, Moon and all the planets
are interdependent.

All of Nature—trees, grasses, insects, animals and people—is part of a greater Whole.

One Truth shines through all Creation.
Rivers, mountains, plants, animals, Sun, Moon, stars, you and I
are all expressions of that one Reality.

Everything that is, exists in the supreme Consciousness.

Lokah Samastah Sukhino Bhavantu—May all beings be peaceful and happy—
is the Hindus' daily prayer.
This ancient chant embraces all of Nature and Creation.
The central message of the Eternal Way of our ancestors is unity in diversity.

Many souls have walked the Earth who experienced this Truth
and many more are yet to come.
Modern science is slowly moving toward the same discovery.

Nature is God in a form that human beings can perceive with their limited senses.

Nature is supreme Consciousness made visible.

In Nature there are no mistakes—
everything has a purpose and nothing is insignificant!

Just as the screws in an airplane are as important as the engine,
everything in Nature counts.

The most insignificant and even seemingly harmful plants and animals
play an active role in Creation and have a specific function.
Spiders manage the insect population, snakes control the rodents,
unicellular plankton feed the whales, and so forth.

Everything in Creation is a deity with special powers.
For every action there is also a deity.

Everything is full of divine Consciousness—nothing is inert.

Everything in Nature is a wonderful miracle.
Isn't the little bird flying through the great sky a miracle?
And the banyan tree growing from a tiny seed?
Think of all the miracles—camels with portable water bags,
kangaroos with attached cradles!

Everything made by God is so precious.

Behold the enormous beauty and perfection of Nature—
everything is so joyful!
All of Creation is rejoicing.

God's earth and Nature's song are perfectly tuned.
Only human beings create cacophony.

The Sun gives us sunlight and the trees give us oxygen
while taking away poisonous carbon dioxide.
Rivers and lakes offer us their thirst-quenching waters.
The air provides our every breath.
Forbearing and forgiving Mother Earth is our constant support.
But do we ever remember to thank her?

In spite of all of Nature's wonderful boons and gifts
mankind relentlessly abuses the Earth.
And still she patiently tolerates us, blessing humanity
with ever more wealth and prosperity.

Children, Nature stands before us as the embodiment of renunciation.
Rivers, mountains, trees—everything in Nature—is a teaching in pure selflessness.

Nature is a text we should study very carefully!

Look at the trees, offering fruit and shade to everyone who passes by.
Even as we cut them down they protect us from the Sun.

The lifespan of a flower is very brief and still it offers its nectar
unreservedly to the enchanted birds and bees.

There is nothing in this world that has not, in one way or another,
nourished our growth.

We should be very grateful since we are indebted to everything in this world.

Today we live in a world that exaggerates the importance of material life
and destroys the beauty and vitality of life.

While we enjoy beautiful landscapes on our walls,
we cut down the forests, fill in the ponds and pollute the sacred rivers.

Nature is the magical bountiful wish-fulfilling Tree
and Man is the Fool sawing off the branch on which he sits.

With reckless abandon and utter disregard for the suffering we cause,
we take more and more from our Mother.

We have become so ignorant we think of Nature as a place
where we can go and take and take and take, and never give anything back.

While the Earth, the trees and the oceans are always serving us,
we incessantly exploit them.

We cannot know the function of everything — Nature is a mystery beyond us.
And still we foolishly keep on destroying animals, plants, trees
and healing herbs we naively consider weeds.

All creatures benefit humanity and have an important role in the world,
however small that may be.
All creatures also need humanity's help.
We depend upon one another for our mutual survival.

One reason for the natural calamities common today
is our limitlessly greedy exploitation of Nature.
We no longer care about the coming generations.
Our ancestors, fully aware of their dependence on Nature,
always left enough for the future before taking what they needed.
Today, however, we only think of *me, me, me.*
The longer we wait to break this mindset and take moral action,
the farther the future recedes into darkness.

In the past twenty-five years we have destroyed forty percent of our forests.
Water and fuel resources keep on diminishing.
Our children and theirs will be the ones to bear the brunt of our actions.

Nature's rhythm depends upon ours, and our health and resilience depend upon hers.
We have no choice but to harmonize with Nature.

If we do not respect Mother Nature,
we can expect more and more natural disturbances.
Since the disappearance of most of the trees, we are already witnessing
irregular insufficient rainfall and erratic patterns of sunlight.

Nature's harmony has been damaged by our indiscriminate behavior.
Climatic patterns have changed, temperatures are warming, rainfall is diminishing
and the seasons are unpredictable.

To live in harmony with Nature we must love all her creatures
and fulfill our own responsibilities.

Our estrangement from the culture of responsibility
has caused all of these irregularities.

Mother Nature has a thousand eyes and ears.

Nature records all our actions.
All our thoughts and words continue in a subtle form.

Nature has a rhythm—the wind, rain, ocean waves, breathing
and heartbeat of the animals all follow her beat.
Our rhythm is determined by our thoughts and actions and when these are disturbed, the
whole rhythm of life is disturbed.

Today, the atmosphere is full of the poisonous gases of our cars, buses and factories.
But the worst pollution of all comes from the selfish wicked thoughts of human beings.

While our streets and houses have grown wider and wider,
our minds and perspectives have grown narrower and narrower.

Morality has become an ancient relic.

In the past we did not need environmental protection
because protection of Nature was inseparable from reverence for God and life.
People loved and served Nature and society rather than worshipped God *per se*
because they saw the Creator through Creation.
We loved, protected and worshipped Nature as the visible form of God.

Creation and Creator are You, energy and existence—
Goddess, Goddess, Goddess.
Creator of the Cosmos, beginning and end—
Goddess, Goddess, Goddess.
The essence of the individual soul and the Earth's five elements—
oh Goddess, Goddess, Goddess!

India's tradition of respect and reverence for Nature and life is very ancient.
Our ancestors built shrines to trees, birds and even vipers.
How ironic that even in India the idea of environmental protection
is considered modern.

Protecting the environment was always part of India's culture
since Nature was viewed as part of God.
When India decided such thinking was primitive
is when our country stopped protecting the environment.
Today's "environmental protection" lacks the reverence that was once its essence.
And so it does not succeed—people do not defile a river they revere.

In the past we did not need to protect Nature
because our way of life protected it.
Worship, cultural customs, respect and reverence for Creation
were an integral part of life.
Taking only what we needed and avoiding exploiting and destroying
was deeply ingrained in everyone.
Today there is no restraint—we take whatever we want
from Nature and our fellow creatures.

When a man chops down a tree, he is making his own coffin.

Steeped in selfishness, people have forgotten that everything we possess
has been given to us by Mother Nature.
Without Nature, we are doomed.

The current generation lives as if we had no relationship to Nature at all—
we are surrounded by artificiality.

Everything we eat and drink is poisoned—nothing is pure.

Not only is our food and water polluted, but also the air.
Our immune systems are weaker, and more and more people need inhalers to breathe.
One day all of us may need air tanks like astronauts in space.
Most people are allergic to something, usually quite minor.
Due to our increasing alienation from Nature, it is harder and harder to survive.

We use artificial fertilizers and pesticides to grow our fruits and grains,
and preservatives to increase their shelf life.

Whether we are conscious of it or not, we are consuming poisons
that generate many new diseases.
The average human life span, formerly over a hundred years, is under eighty
and more than three-fourths of the population is diseased.

It becomes increasingly difficult to produce sufficient food
to meet the rising demands of an ever-exploding population.
Science seeks artificial means such as chemical fertilizers to increase crop yields,
but the nutritional value of fast-growing vegetables is only a third of natural varieties.
As these scientific methods backfire, our longevity is shrinking.

While we increasingly disconnect from Nature, plants and animals disconnect too.
As apartment buildings replace the forests, birds increasingly use plastic and metal
to build their nests—and in the future there may be no trees at all.
Honey bees that flew kilometers from their hives to pollinate fruits and grains
now get lost and die.

With the earth, the air and the water so full of poison
the Holy Cow that once granted any wish is finally drying up.

Oil, food, potable water and unpolluted air and soil are becoming scarcer and scarcer.

Clean air, water and earth are now endangered species.

Meanwhile, the human population keeps on expanding
at an alarming rate!

There is an enormous imbalance in Nature.

In Amma's childhood we applied cow dung to heal our cuts and wounds,
but today such a practice would cause sepsis.
What was once medicine has become poison.

The biggest threat in the world is not a third world war.
It is humanity's increasing alienation from Mother Nature
and Nature's lost harmony.

We have already polluted the air, the food and the water—if we do not stop
exploiting Nature and all life for our immediate selfish gains,
we will destroy the entire world!

When Amma sees people continuing to selfishly exploit Nature, She feels dread.
If we keep on torturing Nature, we will be ruined.
If we do not change Nature will be forced to make us change—
this is the meaning of her retaliatory behavior.

We must wake up, stand up and act now!

Nature is the Goose that lays the golden eggs.
If we kill her and steal all her eggs, we will lose everything!
We must stop polluting and exploiting Mother Nature and start protecting her
if we wish to safeguard our survival and that of coming generations.

To protect Nature, people must first realize
that we are part of Nature.

We need to regain the inner connection we once had and protect Mother Nature.
We must wake up from our deep inertia.

It is the duty of every single human being to protect our oceans,
our seashores, our forests, our mountains and our streams.

We really have no right to assert ownership or authority over anything on Earth.
Millions of people have come and gone claiming this or that to be theirs.
How amused the Earth must be.
We should be grateful for everything we receive.
If we felt gratitude instead of greed we could spare Earth all our pollution.

As a part of the world people have a right
to use Nature's resources to meet their needs—
but we also have a responsibility to support Nature's balance!

Today the Earth's temperature is soaring, the ozone layer is thinning
and more unfiltered rays are reaching us, causing sunburns and cancers,
burning plants and threatening satellites.
We must plant more trees!

Trees provide fruit and shelter, purified air and water, and shade.
We need to educate the younger generation about the importance of planting trees.
Please give children the gift of a sapling!

Natural disasters may be beyond our control—
not entirely preventable regardless of our progress—
but we can definitely reduce the sorrow and misery that we cause.
Protecting Nature is the first step.

Worldly objects are meant to be used and every object has a purpose.
Without this interdependence the world could not exist.
Plants and trees depend on the earth for nutrients;
animals and people depend upon plants and other animals.

The story of this world is one of interdependence.

People used to be content with what they received —
they were happy with little things.
They understood the meaning of sacrifice, simplicity and charity.
Where did we go wrong?

Our main problem lies in our inability to distinguish
between luxuries and needs.

It is fine to take from Nature to meet our basic needs,
but to take more is something very different: It is exploitation.

Wastefulness is a kind of theft from those who need the things we waste.

Any action performed without discrimination is immoral.
Careless extravagance is a sin.

Cutting down trees to build a house is not necessarily wrong,
but cutting down trees indiscriminately and unconsciously is wrong.

We should realize that whenever we take more than we need,
we are taking an extra life, either a plant or an animal.

We may think that since human beings can speak, walk, act, think and feel
and plants cannot, that plants are lifeless and therefore it is all right
to cut, destroy and use them for our own purposes.
But everything in Nature has a purpose to fulfill.
There are no mistakes in Creation—everything is well calculated,
precisely measured and perfectly proportioned.

We may think that destroying a tree or a plant is a lesser wrong
than killing a person, but that is incorrect.
When we selfishly damage a plant, we extend its karma
and block its evolution to a higher form and ultimate liberation.

Everything that exists is a part of life and has the same life purpose.

Children, it is impossible to live without killing—even if we are vegetarian
we kill so many plants to sustain our lives.
Even by breathing we kill many invisible creatures.
It is really our attitude and humility that determine whether we kill.

Plants experience fear and emotion just as we do.
When we approach them with a knife or an axe, they tremble with helpless anxiety.
If we have a subtle mind and an open eye, we can perceive this.
A plant's emotions may be invisible to the senses
but a compassionate heart can feel them.

We are not using the gifts that God has given us
which enable us to think discriminantly and act wisely.

Change takes a lot of effort—but we are too busy to think of others
and have let ourselves become isolated and apathetic.

We possess knowledge but lack awareness.
We possess information but lack intelligent discriminating minds.

There is a very great imbalance now — Nature is in a fierce state
and can no longer cooperate with us.

Concerning Nature's condition, we should be as alert
as if we were standing at gunpoint!

If the air and the water get more polluted and more rivers dry up,
if more and more forests are destroyed and more new diseases keep spreading,
Nature and humanity are in store for a monumental disaster.

Mankind is a walking disaster.

Like a herd of elephants, human beings are trampling Nature mercilessly.

The inner human climate has changed for the worse
and fear and discord are the new normal.

Amidst the agitation created by man's aggressive, wicked ways,
Nature is withdrawing her bountiful blessings.
If we do not change our behavior, we pave the way to our own demise.

Says the pot to the potter: "Today you grind me, but tomorrow I will grind you."

Nature's agitation is obvious
in the water, the soil, the air, the plants, the animals and the people.
Somehow, somewhere, it will all explode.

In Creation, everything has an order and every living being has a role.
Forests, rivers and mountains all have their duties.
Nature stores food for life and recycles waste for its own protection.
But when men selfishly and drastically alter Nature,
she cannot maintain her balance and turns ugly.

When natural tragedies take place, it is not God
who should be cross-examined in the witness box but Man.
Every natural disaster is a warning from Nature that we need to correct
our behavior — a warning that should not be ignored!

As science continues its progress, more cities, factories, over-population
and mountains of waste are on their way.
If we do not consider the needs of Nature, society and future generations,
we will reap, instead of short-term gains, a major tragedy.

Change or death — that is our choice.

Ninety percent of our forests are now gone.
We are at the edge of the irreversible destruction of Nature.

May we never reach the point where humanity has to die
for the rest of the Earth to survive.

May divine Grace save us from the catastrophe we are approaching.

All of Nature, every human mind, is very agitated — only divine Grace can help us.

Only by fulfilling our moral responsibilities,
praying with our hearts
and serving the world with our hands
will we ever be able to restore Nature's balance.

Prayers and meditation have the power to alter the outcome.
We need to make an effort and God's grace will be with us.

Humanity must approach Nature with kindness and consideration.
Not a single creature or human being — nothing! — would exist without Nature.
It is our duty to lovingly care for all living beings.

Every creature, small or large, contributes to Creation.
We must develop the same worshipful attitude our ancestors had
toward Nature and the Earth.

We should not see their culture as primitive but vital to honoring our Mother.
Amma humbly bows to the ancient tradition of the American Indians.
May the entire world emulate their example and the world become a better place.

Whenever we take more than our share from Nature
we deny others their rightful share.
We should take only what we need and try to give something back.

Sharing with others and taking only what we need
is true spirituality.

Whether we write with a hundred-dollar or a thousand dollar pen,
our writing can still be read.
Let us use what we need—and give the rest to those suffering in poverty!
We should avoid luxury.

We spend a lot of money on luxuries and habits detrimental to our health.
If we renounce our selfishness and spend our money on people
who can barely survive, who cannot afford even one meal a day,

we can brighten their lives as well as our own.

When we feel no compassion it is easy to destroy life.
Lack of compassion means that we do not care about other beings
and do not realize that everything is alive.

Life and God are one.

Nothing should ever be totally destroyed.
If we have ten seeds, we should save at least one for planting.
If we make a hundred dollars from the harvest, we should give at least ten to charity.

We did not inherit the land from our ancestors, we borrowed it from our children—
and we have to return it unharmed.

Merely earning money and creating children is not enough—
we need to preserve their future as well.
It is our duty to carefully preserve the world for our children.

We need to remember that everything is sentient, conscious and alive.
There is no such thing as matter—Consciousness alone exists.
When we approach life with this awareness, destruction becomes impossible,
the idea itself dissolves and we can only help and serve others
for the betterment of the world.

When we leave this life, the only thing that will matter
is how little we used of Nature's resources—our carbon footprint—
and how much we did for others—the footprint of our compassion.

We should give as much as we take—this is our God-given human duty.
We have already betrayed the trust of our species—
let us now go forward with faith and Love in our hearts.

Only through Love and respect for Nature will we ever awaken spiritually.
The goal of spirituality is to feel Life everywhere.

To Love means to feel Life in everything.

We will not be admitted to the realm of God without the signature
of the tiniest ant on our application.

We need to cultivate a spiritual culture that respects and worships the sanctity of Life.
There is no other way to save the Earth and the human race.

For our own survival as well as that of generations to come,
we must stop polluting and exploiting Nature.

In our cities the growing number of vehicles
is one of the primary causes of increasing pollution.
If five people ride together, pollution is decreased by eighty percent.
If an entire country car-pools, pollution radically declines, rapidly vanishing oil
is saved, and most importantly Love and cooperation increase.

We should ride bicycles for short distances to get exercise as well as save fuel.
One major cause of increasing illness is lack of exercise.
We can walk and save the expense of a gym.

We need factories, but must find new ways of decreasing their pollution
and locate them far from human habitation.

We cannot escape disease simply by destroying whole populations
of mosquitoes, chickens and cows.

The human race needs to understand
that it is not the only species that has a right to life.
How many species have we already driven to extinction?
We should have compassion not only for humanity but for all of life.

God dwells not only in human beings but also in animals and other species—
mountains and rivers, valleys and trees, birds and clouds,
the Sun, Moon and stars, the moving and unmoving.
God is everywhere.
How can anyone who understands this ever kill and destroy life?

The ancient scriptures of Bharat (India) teach us that the same divinity exists
in a human being, a dog, a cat, a cow, a bird and a plant—in all living beings.

How can we feel anger and hatred when we see divinity
enthroned everywhere in the world?

We have no right to destroy.
Since we cannot create life, we must not destroy it.
God is the creator, the sustainer and the destroyer—these are beyond us.

The Earth cannot be changed for the better unless human consciousness changes.

We can vow to increase our awareness by disciplining our minds
through meditation, prayer and positive thinking.
We can commit ourselves to a global ethic of mutual understanding
and a way of life that benefits society, fosters peace and is Nature-friendly.

Restoring the harmony of Nature should be our first priority.
Every person on this planet needs to play a part.
We should do whatever we can to stop polluting and try to live simply.

If we are willing to take risks and make sacrifices
we can bring about fundamental change.

God has assigned a place to everything in the universe.
There is no such thing as *great or small* — everything is of equal value.
We should have this vision of equality and revere everything as God.

Children, our goal is to feel life everywhere, not to destroy it!
We who cannot create life have no right to destroy it —
only the Supreme creates, preserves and destroys life.
When we do not know what to do, it is wiser to do nothing than to act rashly.

Sincere seekers and believers of Truth never harm Nature.
Seeing Nature as divine, they do not experience her as something separate.
These are the real Nature lovers.

Great Souls would never do anything to hurt anyone
because they realize that everything is one.

In a perfect relationship between humanity and Nature,
a circular energy field is created in which we flow into one another.

When human beings fall back in Love with Nature,
Nature will fall back in Love with us.
She will stop hiding things from us and open her boundless treasure trove
for our enjoyment.

If we make Nature happy with our good thoughts and deeds,
Nature will bless humanity with a lavish harvest.
The universal Mind and the individual mind will overflow as one.

Like a mother, Nature will nourish and protect us.

When we serve Nature, Nature will serve us.
When we protect the animals and the plants, they will naturally protect us.

When we are one with Creation and our hearts are full of Love,
everything becomes our friend and is always at our service.

Life is harmonious
when people move to the beat of Nature.

Modern science shows that trees and plants respond to our thoughts and actions.
Instruments registering the feelings of plants indicate that they suffer
when we are cold-hearted and uncompassionate.
This is why saints and sages have always lead lives of total harmlessness.

The ancient seers of India who delved deeply into their own consciousness
became aware of the feelings of the trees and the plants
and their capacity to express them.
With an attitude of loving-kindness, we too can learn to listen and understand them.

Human beings are not the only creatures gifted with the power of Speech—
animals, birds and plants have this ability too.
Many of us may not understand them, but those who know the pure Self do.

How blissful were the days when Amma lived outdoors.

Strangely, it was the animals that understood and responded to her feelings.
When She cried, they cried; when She sang, they danced.
When Amma fell unconscious, they crawled up on her body.
Once we are liberated from attachment and aversion, we will understand
that everything is of equal value—then, even hostile animals will become friendly.

Learn to enjoy Nature and communicate with her—for she is our real family.

Try to grow your own vegetables organically, spend time with your plants,
talk to them, sing to them and kiss them—and they will reinvigorate you.

We draw spiritual strength, hope and trust from Nature
when we pray, chant and meditate—through both the words and the silence.

Prayers make us stronger.
Chanting prayers generates positive energy that cleanses our cells.
Prayer is a pure thought vibration.

Prayer and spiritual focus are powerful ways to help purify the atmosphere.

Prayer and spiritual practice are more important today
than at any other time in human history.

Unless we practice spiritual awareness in our daily lives
positive change will not and cannot happen.

Through sincere prayer and earnest effort we can invoke divine grace.

Nature registers all our sincere prayers.
When we pray for others, the whole universe prays for us.

Prayer transforms our inner and outer life into music.

When we pray, we are planting seeds of Love.

Prayer is Love—when we pray we spread waves
of pure Love through the world.

Meditation, prayer, chanting and other practices have the power to save us.
Reverence and devotion, developed through faith, is very beneficial
to both humanity and Nature.
Chanting prayers with concentration creates a positive response in Nature
and helps restore harmony on Earth.

The constant stream of Love that flows from a true believer
to all Creation has a gentle and soothing effect.

It is the duty of humanity to serve and take care of Nature
and she in turn will provide us with all we need.

When we approach Nature with Love,
she will become a friend who will never let us down.
When we bow before Existence in pure humility,
the whole universe will bow in service to us.

When we truly love Nature, she becomes our best friend—who needs a spouse?
Like a poet waiting for the next line—nothing else is on our minds.

Human survival depends on countless aspects of Nature
continuously and selflessly serving and supporting us.
Once we realize this, we will appreciate every breath we take.

Once compassion arises and we earnestly seek to serve and protect life,
we will not pick even one leaf unnecessarily.
We will only pick a flower already falling from its stem.

When we live in harmony with Nature, we are happy and content.
When we live in Love and unity with her, we find the strength to overcome any crisis.

Life is complete when humanity and Nature move in mutual harmony.
When our rhythm and melody flow in complementarity,
we create beautiful music like a symphony.

God is the indivisible boundless Oneness.
Nature, the atmosphere, the birds, the animals, the plants and trees—
every atom radiates divine Power.
Divinity resides in every sentient and insentient being.
Once we understand this, we can love ourselves and everything around us.

Life and God are one!

Some people may doubt we possess the power to restore Nature's lost balance
and wonder if we are not too limited.
We are not too limited—we have infinite Power within us!
We are sleeping and unaware of our own strength.
Once we wake up, the Power will rise.

The world is like a lake—
one person alone may not be able to clean it,
but if each does his part, together we will be able to clean and restore it.

Do not be lazy.
Do what you can, and then we will be able
to accomplish what we must.

One day everybody dies—it is unavoidable.
Rather than let these bodies rust from disuse,
let us wear them out in service to the world.

Today's youth are the pillars of tomorrow's world.
They have the potential to make great changes in the world.
Dedicated youth can inspire others by joining together and creating initiatives.
Young energy must be channeled toward a good cause.

Mother says that everyone should plant trees
and encourage the younger generation to plant trees too!

Global warming threatens our very survival.
We can do little to affect the ozone and solar flares, but we can plant trees.

Trees are the air filters of the earth—they purify our air.
We need to plant trees!

Planting trees is a blessing.

If we plant plenty of trees and medicinal plants to cleanse the air
we can avoid so many diseases.

Planting two trees for every tree cut down is not, as some claim, sufficient.
There is a very big difference between what one large tree
and two small trees can provide.

Forests play the most vital role in maintaining Nature's harmony.
Outliving us, they provide fruit and shade for generations to come.
Every nation should protect its remaining forests
and plant as many new trees as possible.
All of us should vow to plant at least one tree a month.

We depend on honeybees for our fruits and vegetables —
but we have damaged their memory with pesticides so they can no longer fly
the distances necessary to collect pollen and return to their hives.
We need to plant more flowering trees and install beehives.

Nature is a vast garden — birds, trees, animals, plants and people are its bright flowers.
When all are vibrating with pure Love, the splendor of the garden will be perfect.

May we all work to prevent the wonderful diversity of the flowers from withering
and dying out — so this vast earthly garden may stay beautiful forever.

Together we can restore the beauty of Nature to the face of the Earth.

Only through Love and compassion are protection and preservation of Nature possible.

Whenever humanity's Love grows, it touches and pacifies Nature.

The best protection of Nature is Love.

It is the urgent duty of every human being to make Nature happy
with loving, faithful, sincere and selfless actions.
Only then, will Mother flow and bless humanity with her never-ending bounty.

There is harmony in the universe.
Everything is connected like a net held by each one of us
and every action vibrates to the farthest reaches.
We should not wait for other people to change but change ourselves
and do whatever good we can.

If we want others to change, we need to first change ourselves.

Do not be downcast, wondering how we will ever clean up all this pollution.
Let each do what he or she can, and the next person do what she or he can.
And if many participate, the pollution will soon be cleaned up.
We must not retreat but make a concerted effort!

On Earth Day everyone should plant saplings.
New houses should be built half the size of current houses to save trees,
water, electricity and other resources.
We should carpool to save fuel.
Thus, one step at a time, we will create change.

If all join together in carpooling, nurturing bees, planting trees, growing vegetables,

cleaning the environment and managing our waste—if all of us get together
and work with real focus, we can transform the Earth into heaven.
But first we must create it within ourselves.
Amma prays that the Supreme will bestow the grace we need.
Amma prays for God's blessing.

Service is the power that sustains the universe.
When humanity serves Nature, Nature serves humanity.
Only service with compassion, kindness, Love and faith will bring about
real peace and happiness.

What are the laws of Nature? Unity, sacrifice and selflessness—
the unified awareness of We.

When people live by Nature's laws, the song of Life is sweet.

May divine Grace guide and save us.

8

SCIENCE WITH SPIRITUALITY

Humanity stands on the threshold of a new era
when science and spirituality will proceed hand in hand.

The merger of science and spirituality will help humanity move
from the dark corridors of the past into the bright light of peace, harmony and oneness.

Joined together, science and spirituality will create a mighty stream
that will wash away human suffering and revitalize humanity.

We can no longer afford to view the two streams of science and spirituality
as flowing at cross-purposes when they are actually complementary.

Spirituality has never been opposed to science.
Indeed, it is itself a science itself: the science of the mind.

Contrary to popular opinion, spirituality is not religion
and not founded on blind faith.
Spirituality is inquiry, exploration and training in understanding the Self.
It proceeds through sincere and unbiased inquiry.

Spirituality is the practical science of life.
It teaches us how to understand the world,
how to live life to the fullest, and fully realize ourselves.

Spirituality is the way to restore our inner connection to the Self.
It teaches us how to live perfectly in the world.

Spirituality and physical life are inseparable.
Spirituality shows us how to function properly in the material world.
It is like a user's guide that teaches us the basics.

Spirituality is a practical approach to life—like learning how to drive properly.

Spirituality is the science that shows how to understand life more deeply,
how to manage the mind and maintain mental balance.

Spirituality teaches us how to master the mind.

Spirituality teaches us how we can meet life's challenges successfully
and experience genuine happiness and contentment.

From spirituality and spiritual masters come the peace and tranquility essential for life.

Spirituality gives us practice in staying firmly rooted in ourselves
and helps us develop the ability to smile at every situation with equanimity.

Spirituality teaches us how to face everything with a smile.

When we know how to swim, swimming in the ocean is a joyful experience,
but when we don't, the waves can be terrifying and we risk drowning.
To ride life's ups and downs, the right knowledge and attitude is necessary.

Gaining spiritual knowledge is the only way to gain the correct perspective on life
and become strong enough to cope with life's hardships.

Spiritual training makes us stronger, provides understanding
of deeper realms of knowledge, and gives us the courage
and serenity to face the major challenges.

Understanding spirituality means understanding the laws of life.

Only if we understand the spiritual fundamentals
can we confidently confront the problems of life and not crumble.
As armor protects a soldier, spiritual wisdom protects us from life's inevitable ordeals.

Like a lightning rod on a roof, spirituality protects us from the shocks of life.

Once we understand the principles, the art and the science of life management,
life becomes a truly joyful celebration.

Once our eyes can pierce the surface of life,
life is suddenly awash with joy.

Spirituality is the science that teaches us to love ourselves
and accept what comes our way.

People who say that spirituality is escapism are stuck in prejudice.
Trying to explain it to them is like holding up a mirror in front of a blind man,
or like trying to wake up someone pretending to be asleep.

Light cannot be explained to those who only know darkness.

Escapism is the way of the cowardly; spirituality is the way of the brave.
True bravery comes with compassion and determination.
With courage and fortitude, we can face anything.

Spirituality is not an escape from life—
it is an inward journey to the very source of our Being.

It is simply wrong to say that religion and spirituality are founded on blind faith
and their principles are unproven, when spiritual masters have conducted
perhaps even more exhaustive research in the inner laboratory of the mind
than physical scientists have conducted on the external world.

Long, long ago sages delved into the mysteries of the Self—the inner core
of life and Love—and discovered its great splendor and glory.
In a state of pure Love, the greatest of all scientists experimented
in the laboratories of pure Being.

The sages of ancient India established and developed the arts and sciences
of linguistics, architecture, astronomy, mathematics, health, diplomacy, economics,
musicology, erotica and logic—and considered each field a stepping-stone to the Truth.

The holy books of India, the Vedas and the Upanishads, are like an ocean
constantly evaporating in the sun to fall as life-nourishing rain.
The great Souls who attained the purest Knowledge still enlighten humanity today
through the messages they left in these texts.

While contemporary scientists burden themselves with more and more facts,
ancient seers immersed themselves in Oneness, emptying themselves
so that Knowledge could readily flow through them.
While modern scientists narrow and circumscribe their point of view,
the ancient seers expanded theirs to embrace the entire universe.
While scientists see the many, sages see the One.
A scientist is a part of existence—a sage is the whole.

A scientist seeks the truth of the empirical world through the analytical method.
Dissecting objects to analyze their functions, he uses animals for research—
not pets—measuring their respiratory rate, blood pressure and pulse,
and in the name of science and truth, cuts them open to examine their organs
and in so doing destroys the very life he studies.

Spiritual science is based on the fundamental principle that all is one.
Spiritual seekers search for what is present and unchanging in everything.
When that is known, everything is known, and nothing else remains to be known.

The Ancients recognized the divine Consciousness in both sentient and insentient life.
And so a tradition of respect and reverence for all of life unfolded.
Temples were built to serpents and birds—spiders and lizards were considered holy.
There was no disrespect or distaste for birds, animals, plants or trees,
since all were seen as a direct manifestation of God.

The Eternal Way teaches us to love all things—that is why our Love for God
is expressed in temple worship dedicated to mountains, rivers, trees,
birds, reptiles and many other creatures.

In her childhood, Amma was taught if She accidentally stepped on cow dung
She should bend over and touch it reverently, since it fertilizes the grass
that feeds the cows that provide the milk that nourishes people.

The hallmarks of ancient Indian culture—full realization of the Self
and pure compassion for all living creatures—are still alive and vibrant today.

Everything in the universe is seen as a different form of ultimate Truth.
That is why we should learn to respect, love and serve even the tiniest of creatures,
since all creatures are one with our Self.

There is a story in the *Bhagavatam* about a God-intoxicated Soul
who adopted twenty-four gurus, including some birds and animals.
This is the attitude all of us should have since all creatures have something to teach us.
Even in apparently inert matter the ancient sages perceived God's presence.
"All is pure Being," they chanted, "all is God's essence."

The Eternal Way does not deny or reject any sphere of life or culture
and encourages all the arts and sciences.
It sees no contradiction between spiritual and worldly life.
There is no rejection of the world in the name of spirituality.
On the contrary, it teaches that spirituality makes life richer and more meaningful.

Thousands upon thousands of Yogis born in India
have lived these principles revealed to the sages long ago —
principles that could greatly reduce our suffering.

Science without spirituality
and spirituality without science are both incomplete.
One of the key reasons for the large number of conflicts in our world
is their separation.

Separating science and spirituality was the great crime of the twentieth century.

When scientific intellect is combined with spiritual awareness,
the result is compassion and sympathy for all.

A scientist should be a lover of humanity, Creation and life.

Life is Love.
A true scientist loves humanity and all of Creation.

Scientific inventions can be very beneficial,
but they should never be allowed to violate Nature.
Modern science has reached amazing heights, but sadly it has lost the ability
to see the whole Truth clearly, and act accordingly.

Advocates of reason may claim that they are right and others wrong,
but those who love never make such claims
because people matter more to them than being right.

May all of us develop minds open enough to embrace both
scientific knowledge and spiritual understanding.

Spirituality is the foundation of all moral values.
There is no more powerful agent for human welfare than knowledge
combined with spiritual values.

Spiritual values guide us and keep us from getting lost and doing wrong.
When we stray, it is our conscience that tells us to stop and return to the path.
If we cannot discriminate between right and wrong,
between the important and unimportant,
knowledge is a flower with no fragrance, a word without meaning,
a flame that gives no light.

The foundation of all values is spirituality.
If we lose our values, we are like satellites that have broken away
from the Earth's gravitational force.

Knowledge is a mighty river that nourishes culture wherever it flows.
But without cultural values, it becomes a force of sheer destruction.

In the beginning of human life, knowledge was meant to elevate humanity.
But since we have used it for selfish purposes instead,
knowledge and discovery have become increasingly destructive.

To say that knowledge is expanding is like saying, "The Sun rose but it is still dark."
Can we really say that science, with all its impressive achievements,
has made humanity any more humane?

Millions of dollars have been spent on exploratory missions into the oceans
and into outer space, but what missions have been undertaken
to explore the world here inside us?

Has science not failed entirely to make humans beings peaceful and happy?

We are Janus-faced: On one side we have science and technology;
on the other, poverty and crimes against women.

The only difference between people in wealthy countries and people in poor countries
is the wealthy cry in air-conditioned rooms in mansions
and the poor on dirt floors in shacks.

The Modern Age has a dangerous tendency to exaggerate the value
of analysis, reason and logic, and neglect the functions
that unite people, namely Love and faith.

While the human intellect has grown stronger, the human heart has atrophied.
Human beings have lost the power of discrimination.

There are two languages spoken in this world—
that of the head and that of the heart.
The voice of the intellect has become deafening!

Intellectual domination has almost completely destroyed the quality of our lives.
Beauty, Love, faith and surrender to a higher good have almost entirely vanished.

The modern mind is dry—parched by too much thinking.
People use their intellect for everything!
Heart, faith and beauty are near extinction.
We must not let the intellect and reason consume our hearts.

Science and reason should not be emphasized to the exclusion of everything else.
They have their place and should stay in it.
The intellect cannot grasp the expansive, boundless nature of life
and cannot comprehend its true meaning.

A predominantly intellectual person cannot acknowledge the enchantment
of a moonlit night—cannot simply appreciate something for what it is.
Compelled to analyze, he must try to find a scientific explanation.
Drinking a cup of coffee or tea, he cannot enjoy its flavor
because his mind is already focused on breeding some new bean or leaf.

Without Love the intellectual completely misses out on life's beauty and magic.
Think of such a life—if indeed it can even be called "a life"
since it is really nothing but a death.

We must drop from our heads into our hearts.

Sometimes humility is more important than intelligence.

Excessive knowledge indicates excessive ego—and what a huge burden that is!

Let us remove the load from our heads, surrender it to a higher Power and be free!

With a big ego, we cannot enjoy the sweetness and beauty of life.
The intellectual sees only the surface, and cannot penetrate the shallows
or dive down into the depths.
Standing on the shore he ponders the origins of the sea
but does not notice the soft caress of the breeze,
the beauty and grandeur of the waves.

Too much intellect has inflated the ego to the point that narcissism
has become a grave problem.

We use our talents and skills to aggrandize ourselves
and do not care how we affect others.

We do not want to be ordinary; we want to be extraordinary—better than others.
Incapable of being happy with ourselves, we want recognition and honor.
All this comes from living more in the mind than in the heart.

The intellect dominates our days and Love has become something rare.
Let us try to empty our intellects of all their useless thoughts
and fill our hearts with Love instead.

We can only receive Love when our hearts are open!

We live in our private worlds and pride ourselves on our individuality
and personal strengths—when we should be enjoying the vast Ocean all around us. *212*

We limit ourselves by only thinking about ourselves.

We are hugging to death a tiny bubble in an endless Ocean.

Immersed in illusion, we confuse the real with the unreal and the unreal with the real.
Viewing life through the eyes of ignorance,
we keep feeding the finite self and neglecting the infinite Self.
Intent on stuffing our egos, we do not even want to know the Self—
which would mean starving the ego.

And the blindness of the ego pushes us ever further into the abysmal darkness
where we suffer and make others suffer too.

Take the most egotistical of men, the world dictators,
who crave only position and power and provoke wars with zero concern
for the peace and well-being of society—even their own wives and children.
Caring only about themselves, they are utterly indifferent to the evil they do,
the negativity they bring wherever they go
and the legacy of misery they leave behind them.

Always tense and fearful, the egotist is never happy or content.
Blinded by all-consuming desire for power, he never hesitates to use
the cruelest and most devious of tactics to grab control—
casually destroying others in the process.
The egotist is forever haunted by the fear of losing his possessions and power.

Scientists become better scientists when they learn to be less egocentric.
Politicians who speak more from the heart than the head
set a better and more inspiring example.
Athletes perform their best when the ego is under control.

The inner truth is only realized when the sense of individuality perishes.

Tadpoles swim in the water thanks to their tails—
but once their tails fall off and they become frogs, they can leap wherever they want.
We human beings are like tadpoles—the ego is the tail that limits our freedom.
Once it is gone we can see ourselves in, and feel compassion for, everything.

Children, learn to live as if you never existed
and then you will live in the Truth.

The ego will eventually destroy us.
To receive grace we need to be dutiful and humble.

The winds of grace can only carry us when we lighten the burden of the ego.

There is something beyond the mind and effort which determines the outcome—
and that is divine grace.

While human effort is in our hands, grace is in the hands of God.

Amma is not saying that we should not make an effort,
but that the power of effort is limited
and only successful when combined with grace.

Keep your ego but learn to master it!
Be considerate of others, for each is a door that opens to God and your true Self.

Imagining that our achievements are due entirely to our own efforts
is like putting salt in milk—it ruins the sweetness.

Whatever we do, numerous factors over which we have no control
also influence the outcome.
Only grace from beyond has the power to align all the factors in our favor.

Grace comes from beyond and is limitless.

We really know nothing.
Everything is controlled by the Supreme.
Like logs floating in the water we are helplessly carried downstream.
Only when the ego becomes a floating corpse, will the Sun of Knowledge rise.

When we spend our life learning everything we can
about the external world and other people's lives,
we miss the most obvious and wonderful world of all: Our Self!

We identify with the seen rather than the Seer.

Knowledge of the external world is ignorance, say the timeless Vedas and Vedanta.
Spiritual knowledge makes clear Who We Are.

Life is not a machine—it is Consciousness!

All of spirituality is contained in this single word: Consciousness.

The mind is darkness and Consciousness is the light.
In the light of Consciousness, we can see life as it truly is.

Spirituality and science exist on different planes—
spirituality picks up where science leaves off.

Science is still searching for the cosmic Intelligence,
but until it strikes a balance with spirituality it will never discover
that life-giving principle forever beyond the intellect.
The overlooked interior has to be explored if we are ever to understand
what lies behind the face of the world.
Only when we function from our hearts will we ever be able
to see and feel that divine Power.

Search for the answers that you cannot find in science in spirituality.

Experience is the true master.

The ancient seers understood from experience
that the basis of all knowledge is the Consciousness within us.
Today this Knowledge must be integrated with the discoveries of modern science.

Knowledge is limitless—its possibilities are vast as the universe.
To know whether a discovery is beneficial or detrimental
it must be contemplated with a meditative mind.

Life is a journey from consciousness to Consciousness—
a return to the origins of our existence.

Creation is not an accident.
The Sun, the Moon, the oceans, the trees, the flowers,
the mountains and the valleys are not accidents!
Planets circle the Sun without slipping an inch from their orbits.
Oceans cover vast areas of the Earth without ever swallowing it up.
If this beautiful Creation were simply an accident, it would not be so orderly
and systematic—it would be chaotic!

Everything that occurs has a cause—nothing is accidental.

Behold the enthralling beauty of Creation!
How could we ever consider this an accident?
The cosmic pattern of beauty and order pervading all of Creation
makes it strikingly clear that behind it all, there is a great Heart and Intelligence.

We say that a computer has two parts:
the external visible hardware and the internal invisible software.
In reality, they are not separate since neither can function without the other.
This is analogous to the visible world of diverse names and forms
and its invisible inner power.
The visible world all around us is merely the hardware.
The unified consciousness and power that connect everything we can see
and make it work perfectly, is like the software in a vast computer network
which we call *Consciousness* or *God*.
Whatever is happening, we should be aware of this Power.

Today we live in a quick-fix world, increasingly addicted to science and technology.
It is crucial that we not forget the real purpose of life
which is to experience and share Love.
We need to lovingly consider the world of people and Nature around us
and take the time to look within and find out who we are.
We are sources of radiance with the power to shine like the Sun!

The intellect comes from the mind.
Love comes from the heart.
When we use them together we will discover the Truth.

When we ask for a new truth, we are like a kindergartner asking his teacher:
"Miss, you've been saying 'two and two is four' so long, it's getting old—
can't you say something new like 'two and two is five'?"
Truth cannot be changed.
It is, was and always will be the Truth.

Humanity does not need a new truth—
it only needs to recognize the one that already exists, now and forever,
the one that is never old and never changes,
the one and only Truth that is always new and always the same.

The Truth does not exist in separate drops, even though it seems to.

We need to see the Truth that shines in all things eternally.

One Truth shines through all of Creation.
The rivers, mountains, plants, animals, Sun, Moon and stars, you and I
are all expressions of that one Reality.
Many have walked the Earth who have experienced this Truth—
and many more are yet to come.

Modern science is slowly edging its way toward the same discovery.
Reality is an infinite shoreless Ocean and each of us is a wave in that Ocean.
All of us are embodiments of one supreme Reality.

Today scientists say that everything consists of Energy.
Humankind's increasing scientific knowledge will ultimately point to the Supreme.

In the new millennium there will a great spiritual awakening in the East and the West.
This is what the present age demands.
The knowledge that humanity keeps gaining will inevitably lead us to God.

There is no new spiritual message to deliver.
Everything is God—there is nothing but God.
This is the only message.

Messages from Amma

JANINE CANAN MD, **psychiatrist and poet, graduate of Stanford University _with distinction_ and New York University School of Medicine, has followed Mata Amritanandamayi for three decades and authored many books of poetry, translations, anthologies, stories and essays, including compilations of Amma's teachings — the award-winning _Messages from Amma: In the Language of the Heart, Garland of Love,_ and _Love Is My Religion._**

PRAISES FOR AMMA

"God's Love in a human body." —CONSERVATIONIST JANE GOODALL

"A supernova of spirituality!" —*HINDUISM TODAY*

"Like a Mother, Amma loves unconditionally and serves expediently."
— COMEDIAN RUSSELL BRAND

"Amma has done more than many governments have done for their people."
—NOBEL PEACE LAUREATE MUHAMMAD YUNUS

"Truly a saint." —UNITED NATIONS PARTNERSHIPS

"This celestial being who walks among us!" —AUTHOR WAYNE DYER

"The darkness cannot compete with Her." —ACTOR JIM CARREY

"The embodiment of pure Love—Ammachi heals." — AUTHOR DEEPAK CHOPRA MD